WEST TEXAS
Christmas
STORIES

*Edited by*

# Glenn Dromgoole

# WEST TEXAS CHRISTMAS STORIES

ACU
PRESS

Copyright 2013 by Glenn Dromgoole

ISBN 978-0-89112-333-0
LCCN 2013020046

Printed in the United States of America

LIBRARY OF CONGRESS CATALOGING-IN-PUBLICATION DATA
West Texas Christmas Stories / edited by Glenn Dromgoole.
    pages cm
  ISBN 978-0-89112-333-0
  1. Short stories, American--Texas. 2. Texas, West--Fiction. 3. Christmas stories. I. Dromgoole, Glenn, editor of compilation.
  PS558.T4W47 2013
  813'.01089764--dc23

                                                                2013020046

Cover design by Greg Golden
Interior text design by Sandy Armstrong

For information contact:
Abilene Christian University Press
1626 Campus Court
Abilene, Texas 79601

1-877-816-4455 toll free
www.abilenechristianuniversitypress.com

# Contents

Introduction

Following the Star ............................................................ 9
Paul Rowan

Muzzie's Tree .................................................................. 15
Richard H. Brussow

The Tallest Tree in West Texas ..................................... 19
Jane Roberts Wood

Christmas at The Ritz .................................................... 23
Jim Richmond

The Quarter of Remembrance ....................................... 33
Mike Cope

The Big Stocking ............................................................ 39
Tumbleweed Smith

A Little Something Extra ............................................... 43
Jodie Wankowski

I Give You a Star ............................................................ 45
James Bruce Frazier

A Shotgun and a Bird Dog ............................................ 53
Bob Green

Giving Thanks for Small Gifts ...................................... 57
Charlena Chandler

Don't Give Me a Fruitcake for Christmas ..................... 61
Glenn Dromgoole

Denominational Decorating ........................................... 63
Doug Mendenhall

Wages for a Hired Hand ................................................ 67
David R. Davis

The Nomad Princess Christmas ..................................... 75
Reba Cross Seals

Christmas Comfort ......................................................... 81
Carlton Stowers

**Christmas at the Ranch**............................................ 85
*Elmer Kelton*

**A Cowboy's Christmas Blessings**........................... 89
*Natalie Bright*

**Christmas at War**................................................... 95
*Don Knecht*

**Christmas in Jail**................................................... 97
*Rick Smith*

**A Coat for Christmas**............................................ 101
*Betty Davis*

**A Coconut for Christmas**...................................... 105
*Frank Grimes*

**A Corn Shuck Christmas**...................................... 111
*Jack Boyd*

**Faded Mistletoe**................................................... 117
*Jacqueline Siglin*

**The Solo Must Go On**............................................ 121
*John Erickson*

**More Than a Meal**................................................. 125
*Loretta Fulton*

**Uncle Cecil**........................................................... 129
*Don Newbury*

**Chestnuts Roasting**.............................................. 135
*Marla Cooper*

**The Santa Claus Bank Robbery**............................ 139
*A. C. Greene*

**Fire Truck Santa**.................................................. 143
*Burle Pettit*

**Santa Claus a Baptist?**......................................... 147
*Beth Pratt*

**The First Time I Saw Santa**.................................. 151
*Glenn Dromgoole*

**Merry Christmas Amigos**..................................... 155
*Author Unknown*

**Stable Gifts for Today: A Benediction**................. 157

# Introduction

Christmas is our most cherished holiday, or as the song says "the most wonderful time of the year," for many reasons. Christmas tugs at the heart. Christmas evokes memories. Christmas is a time for laughter and joy. Christmas is about faith and family and friendship, about Jesus and also Santa Claus, about giving and receiving, about anticipating and experiencing.

And Christmas is about story-telling. Every one of us probably has a Christmas story or two worth telling—the time when everything turned out perfect, or not; the best Christmas ever; a remembered disappointment; a spiritual encounter; a lesson observed and woven deep into the fabric of our own personal quilt of values; an incident so funny you still laugh out loud years later recalling it.

The stories here, I hope, do all of the above—and maybe more. Some of them may elicit a smile or a chuckle, others may find you wiping away a tear, while others may cause your mind to drift back to moments and memories catalogued deep within your soul. Some are by writers who may be familiar; others by writers you haven't read until now. Some are fiction, others non-fiction, though in the spirit of Christmas it may not always be possible to separate one from the other, especially when it comes to story-telling.

Though very diverse, the pieces in this book have a few things in common. Geography, for one—they are either set in West Texas or they are the product of West Texans putting pen to paper or, more likely, fingers to computer keyboard. Length, for another—none of these stories take very long to read. And, finally, all are intended to help make this Christmas a little more meaningful.

Happy reading, and Merry Christmas.

*Glenn Dromgoole*

*Paul Rowan is a native Texan now based in Vancouver, Canada. His abiding admiration for the people of West Texas was formed many years ago when he spent two years as a writer/editor at the* San Angelo Standard-Times *and twenty, off and on, at the* Fort Worth Star-Telegram.

# Following the Star

by Paul Rowan

It was the meanest blue norther anybody had ever seen. It was so sudden that crows froze in mid-flap and dropped out of the sky like big black hailstones. It froze an animal's exhalation, which then had to be broken off like a twig.

It came so fast no one was prepared. But the kids had been promised ribbon candy and exotic nuts and almonds in the shell, and these things they would have. The man tried to wait it out, hoping forlornly that something might change, but the weather is the weather and will do what it will. On Christmas Eve, with no water in the radiator, he decided to take the mare to the store. The woman tried to talk him out of it: it was too cold, too far, too late in the day. But he would not be dissuaded.

It wasn't far, maybe five or six miles to the south, as the crow flies, but Coke Stevenson used to tell about the lawyer who asked a witness just how far away he was when he saw the alleged crime done by his client, "as the crow flies." "Can't rightly say," said the witness. 'I've never flown with a crow."

In West Texas, distances are deceivingly relative. On a fine April morning, five or six miles is one thing; on a mid-August afternoon or a cold Christmas Eve, quite another. He bundled up as much as he could, noted that the sky was clabbering up for a little something, and set out.

The storyteller paused, stuck the pipe between his teeth and drew three or four times, just enough to keep it going. To his surprise, the children were actually listening to his story. They hadn't even interrupted to ask who Coke Stevenson was. They had asked for a story about Christmas in the olden times, with only two expectations: that it be about something they knew, and that it be true. West Texans are not much on artifice.

You can wager that someone once found sweet water at Sweetwater, and someone once crossed over a stinking creek at Stink Creek. Probably no chamber of commerce at Stink Creek.

He continued.

Getting there was pretty easy. Horse and man arrived cold, but optimistic. He warmed himself by the fire, bought the last of the oranges and apples and nuts and ribbon candy, added the supplies they were running short of, the flour and sugar and coffee and such, tied it all to the reluctant horse and set out for home.

It had turned colder. The path now was dark as the tomb of Annabel Lee. A light snow began to flutter down, perfectly vertically, not horribly horizontally, the way it can in a strong wind.

He began to wonder if he could find his way now, in such conditions. In the night sky, one constant remains. The North Star seems to stand still while the rest of the heavens march around it. They don't, but it appears so. Find the big dipper, follow the two stars that form the front upwards, and there will be the North Star. The man found the star and steered that way exactly, towards the children, the woman, and home.

He grew numb, and then he grew number. He lashed his left hand to the saddle horn and his right foot to the stirrup; they might find him frozen solid, but he would still be atop a fine horse. His mind began to wander. Then a strange thing happened. His focus returned and he saw a bright light bobbing up and down in the distance, like a ship's lights bob just as it comes over the horizon. Then he realized the light was not bobbing up and down; he was. The mare had seen the light too and had broken out of her sullen stumble and now trotted, cantered toward the light, toward warmth, toward home.

Every kerosene lamp and every candle in the house was full ablaze. The woman knew he and the horse were too stubborn to just quit, so she had made their home an easy place to find. She was waiting at the window and ran out into the cold when the horse and man appeared. She helped unlash him from the saddle, a simple chore now far beyond his own fingers, and half-dragged him in to the fire. She began rubbing his hands until he clenched his teeth to stop them from rattling and said, slowly and carefully, "The horse first." She went back into the night and led the horse to its comfort. She took off the saddle and put on the blanket and hugged her neck for a long moment, then returned to the man.

She rubbed his hands and feet and gave him a cup of lukewarm coffee with two spoons of sugar. She wrapped him in blankets and then got inside the blankets herself to add her warmth. Slowly, circulation returned, right down to his little toes.

They started to doze off. She bestirred herself to pack four boxes, two big ones with the children's names and two smaller ones for her and the man, and then they slept, still by the fire. But not for long. The excited chattering of the children woke them early. They could not contain themselves, not with these treasures. There were oranges from Edinburg and nuts from Brazil and ribbon candy from heaven knows where. There was at least an apple and a half for everyone; by popular vote, the mare got a full share. Then and for many years thereafter it was considered the best Christmas ever.

The storyteller paused. He raised his pipe and puffed a couple of times, but the fire was cold. He slapped both hands on his knees and rose.

He was almost to the door when one of the older boys, much given these days to Euclidean geometry and Aristotlian logic, spoke up.

"Wait a minute, wait a minute," he said. "didn't you say it was snowing?"

"Yep," said the storyteller, "that it was."

"Then it doesn't make any sense. If it was snowing then there had to be a cloud cover, and if it was cloudy how could he find a star to steer by?"

The start of a smile began to curl the corners of the storyteller's lips.

"Well," he said, "I guess that's just a pure mystery now, isn't it?"

Published by permission of the author

*When the* Abilene Reporter-News *invited readers to share a favorite Christmas story, this one by Richard H. Brussow of Clyde was so good it ran on the newspaper's front page on Christmas Day. Brussow passed away in 2000.*

# Muzzie's Tree
by Richard H. Brussow

It must have been fate that put this particular fir tree in our yard.

We were visiting my parents in Haltom City. It may have been Thanksgiving, but the weather was mild. My late father decided to do some yard work. There were two small fir trees that had no place in his sculptured landscape. My wife decided to help.

You might say Jeanne was a tree freak. Even to this day the property is cluttered with trees. So it happened that these two fir trees were wrapped in burlap, set in cans, and put in the back of the station wagon for the trip to Clyde.

The next day these two tiny trees were placed in our orchard. Eighteen inches of sturdy fir in one place; less than a foot of puny fir nearby.

It was a brutal winter after the surprisingly mild autumn, with almost a solid week of below-freezing temperatures. Only the tiny tree survived, and it became known as "Muzzie's tree." Over the years the tree grew slowly, but grow it did.

Over these same years Jeanne was diagnosed with cancer, and chemotherapy became a part of the routine.

By 1989, "Muzzie's tree" was perhaps eight feet tall, and Jeanne loved visiting "her" tree. When she was able, this was almost a daily ritual.

Perhaps we all realized this would be her last holiday season. At any rate, Dr. Victor Hirsch, in his wisdom and compassion, scheduled Jeanne's chemotherapy for mid-December so she could enjoy Thanksgiving and Christmas at home.

For some reason I got out the ladder and decorated "Muzzie's tree," but it remained dark for several days. When I brought Jeanne home it was dusk-dark, and as usual the porch light was on. The carport light wasn't, as sometimes happened.

After Jeanne was settled in bed, I went to the kitchen supposedly to fix supper. Instead, I slipped over to flip on the carport light, which had been wired to light "Muzzie's tree." Then I went back in the bedroom and asked what the glare was in the orchard.

The oleander bushes blocked her view so she insisted on going out to be sure it wasn't a grass fire. After bundling up, she took her cane in one hand and my arm with the other and headed for the orchard. At the end of the driveway she could see the glare came from the lights on "her" tree.

Jeanne turned and looked at me with tears in her eyes. Then she dropped my arm, threw down her cane, and walked out to gaze at "her" tree. I followed, and anyone who thinks I didn't have tears in my eyes is a fool! I have tears in my eyes as I write this.

After a few minutes Jeanne turned and threw her arms around me and whispered, "Thank you."

Those two simple words are the most magnificent Christmas present I have ever received because it was, indeed, Jeanne's last Christmas tree.

Reprinted by permission, Abilene Reporter-News

*In her acclaimed novel* The Train to Estelline, *Jane Roberts Wood describes a scene in 1911 where the new seventeen-year-old teacher at the rural White Star school enlists help in finding a Christmas tree for the school on the barren West Texas ranchland.*

# The Tallest Tree in West Texas

by Jane Roberts Wood

I'm so happy about Christmas, and Josh Arnold is the reason for it. Although he and I have had our differences, I decided it would be better if we could be friends. He is often at the Constables, and they, every one of them, speak of him with admiration and respect. So on Saturday morning, when Josh stopped by, I made every effort to be friendly.

The middle of the morning, I was drawing water for the Saturday wash when Josh, who by then had visited everyone in the Constable family, wandered out to the well.

"Let me do that, Lucy," he said, and I stood back, watching him draw up bucket after bucket of water, splashing each into the washtub I had brought from the house.

"Christobel told me you want a Christmas tree for the schoolhouse," he said when he had filled the tub.

"Oh, I do. Why some of the White Star children have never seen a real tree," I said, and the remembered smell of pine and fir sliced through the acrid odor of the rag-weed that grows in clumps all around the well. "If we only had a tree. And a piano!" I added.

Josh threw back his head, laughing, and the sound was not unpleasant. "Good Lord, Lucy! These people don't have enough food to eat, they're parching corn to use for coffee, and you want them to buy a piano! How in the world can they do that?"

"A tree then. I'd settle for a tree," and I looked across the pasture at the thinly-branched mesquite, thought of the scrub oak growing down the canyon walls, and knew there was nothing out here that would reach even half-way up to the ceiling.

"Lucy, you come with me. Come on," and his smile was contagious. "I'll find you a tree." As I hesitated, thinking of the wash, he said, "Come on, Lucinda. Get in the car, and we'll drive until we find the prettiest tree in Hall County."

Enticed by his smile, beguiled by the idea of a tree, I ran to get my cloak, and by the time I reached the car, he had already cranked it and was waiting to help me in. When we reached the middle of the canyon bridge he stopped the car and we looked down, down into the dry canyon dotted with oak which, from the bridge, looked like small green balls. "See anything?" he asked.

"Josh, a Christmas tree should reach the ceiling," I said, shaking my head. "Those scrub oaks are only about three feet tall."

"We'll find a tall one," he said, smiling. "If it's a tall one you want, we'll find it!"

When we reached the fence line of the Constable farm, he stopped again. "Lucy, I think we've found our tree," he said, but I saw nothing more than a fence piled high with tumbleweeds.

Those grow everywhere out here. Green in the summer, they turn a silvery gray after the first frost, then break off, and are tumbled by the wind for miles across the prairie until they are stopped by some stationary object, usually a fence. At recess, my students and I sometimes race the tumbleweeds, or run to grab them from the wind.

Josh plucked from the fence a car full of the biggest tumbleweeds, and we drove to the schoolhouse.

"Lucy, in ten minutes you will have the tallest tree in West Texas," he said.

And in less than that, Josh had fashioned a tree as delicate as a spider's web, the tumbleweeds' fine network of branches holding them, however they were placed, together. He worked until the tree was taller than he could reach and, standing on a chair, he placed a perfectly round ball of a tumbleweed at its very top.

"Now," he said when he'd finished, "it needs—what does it need?" And I laughed at the perplexity in his voice.

Caught up in his excitement, I said, "Why, cranberries and popcorn. It needs color."

"Berries! Let's go find some berries," he said, and we walked over to the river. There we found, not red, but berries silvered purple, and pale green, and white—enough for lavish garlands for the tree. And after dinner, Christobel, digging around in her ribbon box, found a spool of green plain ribbon, enough for two dozen bows for the tree.

Now I cannot wait for Monday. The students will be so happy.

If we just had a piano, what a splendid Christmas it would be.

Reprinted by permission, University of North Texas Press

Jim Richmond, an Abilene bank president, grew up in Midland and has lived nearly all of his life in West Texas. This story concerns an unforgettable incident at Christmas time during his childhood days in Midland.

# Christmas at The Ritz

by Jim Richmond

Christmas season in the West Texas town of Midland in 1960 was vastly different than a typical Christmas season is anywhere today.

In 1960, malls were still trapped on the drawing board of some young forward thinking architect so that meant all the shopping was done downtown. It meant elaborate Christmas wreaths draped across street light posts and traffic light wires. It was an era when colorful lights were used instead of the more popular white lights of today and every store window was adorned with these lights, candy canes, and garlands and the store owners proudly displayed their goods hoping to lure you inside their stores to spend part of your hard-earned wages.

It was an era when it was still perfectly fine to wish your neighbors a "Merry Christmas" and, regardless of religious belief, your neighbor accepted it as a kind, well-meaning greeting appropriate for the season.

Among the biggest gift kids could ask Santa to bring them was a bicycle or a Lionel train set or maybe a Barbie Doll or an E Z Bake Oven. The parents hoped for one of the new Polaroid Land Cameras or a new transistor radio but mostly they hoped their family enjoyed the Christmas holidays that were spent together.

In the Christmas season of 1960 I was almost six years old and I accompanied my brother Neil, sister Mary, and Mom and Dad on a family shopping trip to downtown Midland. A typical Christmas shopping trip for us in those days meant turning the three kids loose to browse the windows and aisles of the stores while Mom and Dad observed the toys and other items we admired most. Then we would be shuffled back to the car while Mom and Dad, on behalf of Santa, scooped up one item for each of us and hauled the goodies back to the car. Mom would approach the car first while Dad followed slightly behind with the gifts and stuffed them in the trunk while Mom kept us distracted.

However, 1960 was a little bit different for me. For at least one Saturday in late December of 1960, my Christmas shopping trip took a very "Hitchcockian" twist.

Most of the stores we frequented in Midland in 1960 were within about a four block radius. The store I remember most is the J. C. Penney store. It was a two-story building and, if you purchased something downstairs, the ticket would go into a vacuum tube and be sent up to the second floor to accounting. The accounting department would do what they do which is, I was told at the time, "account," and send the tube back. It was an amazing apparatus to me and I always hoped Mom would buy something, even just a pair of socks, so I could see that tube fly up to the second floor of that building. That was probably like the Internet to those employees and it was like rocket science to this little five "going on six" year-old boy.

That December day in 1960, after the five of us had roamed the aisles of J. C. Penney for about ten minutes, Dad called us all together and said it was time for my brother and sister and me to leave so they could do the shopping. As a special Christmas gesture Dad told us that, this time, we could go down the street to the Yucca Theater and take in the special holiday showing of "Pinocchio."

In 1960, without the advent of malls, these theaters were downtown amongst the other stores and these theater operators were no fools. They knew that the typical family had the same drill as us and that the kids would have to wait safely somewhere while their parents shopped. It might as well be in their comfortable theater seats with popcorn and sugary soda in hand. It was a real treat for us, and I remember being surprised that Dad had allowed what, for us at the time, was a huge extravagance.

Before he could change his mind, my sister Mary and I bolted for the door while my brother Neil, who was twelve years old and just one year away from buying his first car, received the necessary funds to facilitate this trip to see the story about the little wooden boy with the long nose and propensity to tell falsehoods. We both hit the glass doors leading to the streets at the same time and then, as if we were suddenly tethered, we stopped and waited patiently for Neil to catch up and escort us to our destination.

To this day I'm not certain exactly when the plan changed for Neil or if he always only had one plan but, as we approached the Yucca Theater, he asked us to wait for him while he got the tickets. He waited impatiently in line amongst a sea of kids and parents. Finally, I saw him reach in his pocket and retrieve some money he then pushed through the box office window. He came back and informed us that, unfortunately, the movie was sold out except for one ticket and the ticket could only be used by a girl. That meant no "Pinocchio" for me or him. Clearly, my sister would be using this ticket. I blindly accepted the notion that the ticket could be gender-intended and my exuberance was drained from me as I watched the single ticket transfer from his hand to hers. The smile on her face was enough to satisfy me, though, and I just looked at Neil and asked, "What are we going to do?" He quickly responded, "Follow me." He never hesitated.

We walked to the end of the block, around the corner, and over a block to the Ritz Theater. The marquis lights weren't flickering. There was no bustling of children around the ticket window. No line of cars to pick up sticky, excitable children from the movie. I didn't see any of that. What I did see was the name of the movie on the marquis. "Psycho" was spelled out in what seemed to me to be huge letters with half as big letters under the title spelling out the names of the stars. "Anthony Perkins" and "Janet Leigh." This was clearly not a Disney movie.

Neil grabbed my hand and crouched down in front of me and said, "We're going in to see this movie." By now "Psycho" had been in town for a couple of months and was near the end of its run. I knew who Alfred Hitchcock was. I knew this would be scary for me.

"I'm scared," I told Neil.

"Don't be scared. What are you, four years old?" he said. "Besides, this isn't as scary as 'Pinocchio.' Pinocchio is like Frankenstein. Some creepy guy creates a kid out of wood that does everything he tells it to and has a nose that grows into the length of a sword anytime he wants it to. Heck, this is actually LESS scary than the movie Mary is at. Besides, I'll tell you when to cover your eyes if I think it will scare you, AND I'll buy you a box of candy, popcorn, and a Coke." Suddenly, all of this seemed like a good idea and I appreciated him rescuing me from the horrors of the Pinocchio movie. He bought the tickets.

As we entered the theater I noticed that it was about half full and most of the people in the movie were middle-aged men. The movie had been out a while but this was Saturday afternoon and some men didn't like to shop for Christmas. I followed Neil to our seats. We kept going down the aisle until we got to the very front row and sat in the center section in the center seats. It was like it was our own little movie. I was scared yet proud to be with my older brother. I knew he would protect me if I got too frightened. After all, he was twelve years old. That seemed ancient to me.

The cartoon came on, a preview or two, a newsreel about the exploits of young President Kennedy and a Merry Christmas wish from Mr. Alfred Hitchcock himself. Then, "PSYCHO."

I tried to be brave, I really did. Even the music frightened me, though. The idea that this woman would intentionally steal money from her boss frightened me. Who would do something like that? Later in the movie came

Anthony Perkins. Enough said. He's scary. Every time he came on the screen I covered my eyes because his eyes were just so haunting looking. I wanted "Pinocchio" in color, not beady eyes in black and white. I tried to turn my attention to my popcorn, candy, and Coke. I couldn't panic in front of Neil. I had to remain calm.

The famous shower scene came about midway through the movie. Scariest thing I had ever seen. The viewer never saw Janet Leigh get stabbed but there was the knife, the curtain was torn, some dark fluid was running down the drain. Yep, something bad happened. I was sure of that. I turned away. Neil forgot to remind me because he was totally involved in the movie by this point. My five-year-old mind was fully aware that my safety net of Neil telling me to cover my eyes was now out the door. I decided I could probably follow the seriousness of the scene based on the sound of the music.

For the next several minutes I became more comfortable but the shower scene remained fresh on my mind. My comfort level recovery was short-lived. There was the scene where Perkins went up to his mom's room to talk to her. My creepiness meter reached the red zone. I covered my eyes with my hands and attempted to cover my ears with my arms at the same time.

By now, my five-year-old legs were nervously rocking and my mind was geared for anything scary. I knew I was on the verge of panic. I looked up at Neil and he was comfortably chomping on his popcorn and slurping his soda. I got very little comfort from that. Neil's popcorn eating image wasn't as comforting as Anthony Perkins' knife-wielding, wide-eyed image was frightening. To say I was a big bag of scared is a huge understatement.

I slumped down in my seat and tried to think happy, comforting thoughts like Santa coming in just a week or so. Reindeer, candy canes, a train, a big guy in a red suit. This seemed to be working. I tried to think of more Christmas comforts. Snow, Christmas lights, our tree with silver tinsel hanging on the limbs, presents under the tree . . . and then . . . BOOM! . . . . We're back in Anthony Perkins' mom's room. Her chair turns around and BOOM! SHE'S A SKELETON! Breaking point.

As fast as I could I sought the last bastion of safety I could think of. I couldn't run out and embarrass myself and Neil so I quickly turned around and put my head in my seat. I wanted none of this.

The problem was that I was so anxious to whirl around and put my head in my seat I had jammed it in so deep that my head was now wedged between the folding seat bottom and the seat back. Each time I tried to pull back, the seat bottom would close and trap my head against the seat back. Yep, it was clear to me. The old skeleton lady had clearly bounced off the screen with knife in hand and was forcing me to stay in my seat by holding my head.

I began screaming at the top of my lungs. "HELP! SHE'S GOT ME! HELP! SHE'S GOING TO KILL ME!" Neil bolted from his seat and began trying to hush me and release me at the same time. Popcorn, Cokes, and Milk Duds flew around like feathers in a West Texas wind storm. I screamed louder.

By about the third round of screaming the lights in the theater were all on and the two theater ushers were on the front row working furiously to release me from the folding chair.

I screamed as loud as I could. "GOD HELP ME! NEIL HELP ME! SANTA HELP ME!" I was clearly desperate at this point, but it would have been fine with me if the big fat man in the red suit swooped down and rescued me. Finally, I was released. I ran out of the fully lit theater to the sarcastic applause and laughter of around a hundred movie patrons.

I was too embarrassed to return to my seat even though I later peeked in and the movie was back on and the lights were off. I decided to wait it out in the lobby. In a few minutes the crowd started filing out and my brother was trailing behind. The relief of being freed had now turned into total humiliation and I dreaded facing Neil after embarrassing him so badly in the movie.

When he emerged from the theater and approached me in the lobby all I could say was, "I'm sorry."

He put his arm around me and said, "Hey that's okay. I think everyone thought you were just part of the entertainment and were supposed to do that to make it seem scarier to the audience. Heck, you're like a movie star."

I smiled as we walked out of the lobby and onto the street.

As we headed back to the Yucca Theater to meet my sister where she and the other "Pinocchio" patrons would soon be exiting through the doors, Neil kept his hand on my shoulder. I felt comfortable and a little less embarrassed, although I was unconvinced that anyone actually thought my outburst was planned by theater management.

We walked to the end of the block and, about halfway back to the car, Neil stopped and knelt in front of me again and said, "Let's keep all this between us, okay?"

"Sure," I said.

"One more thing," he added. "When you're in trouble like you were in the theater it's a good thing to ask for help and to ask God for help but, in the future, I wouldn't put too much faith in any idea that Santa is going to show up and rescue you."

Published by permission of the author

On Christmas morning 1994 Mike Cope preached this family story as his sermon at Highland Church of Christ in Abilene.

# The Quarter of Remembrance

by Mike Cope

I actually got to meet Dr. Channing Barrett, but I don't remember the meeting because I was too young. But that doesn't change my picture of him as a young man walking a marathon of miles every weekend. In my mind I see him returning home to Blissfield, Michigan, around the turn of the century.

Channing Barrett was one of eight boys and was the first ever in the Barrett family to go to college. From his medical school, he walked twenty-five miles home each weekend, always returning a couple days later with clean clothes, a food packet, and a dollar. That dollar might have been a bill, but in my mind it was four quarters.

Dr. Barrett became one of the first ob-gyns in Chicago, practicing at Cook County Hospital. He was known widely both for his innovative surgical techniques and for his ambidextrous skills that allowed him to change hands during long procedures.

There was no patient whom he wouldn't accept. He delivered many "tenement babies" for fifty cents and many babies for the wives of Mafia dons for a good bit more!

With a growing, respected medical practice, a wonderful wife and three children, this young physician seemed to be living the idyllic life. He enjoyed riding horses, lifting weights, and was an early member of the Polar Bear Society—that unique group that takes to the chilly waters of Lake Michigan in January each year to prove—well, who knows what they're trying to prove?

And then World War I interrupted this Norman Rockwell life. Dr. Barrett left Chicago to run a field hospital in France, followed shortly by his seventeen-year-old son, who fought in the trenches.

As long as he could, Barrett sent money back to his wife and daughters. But by the last year of the war, his funds were nearly exhausted. He had no more to mail home. Mrs. Barrett sold most of what they owned, trying desperately to keep her daughters fed and clothed without having to sell the house.

By the time Christmas rolled around in 1918, there were no presents to place under the tree. They were lucky to have a place to live.

But Mrs. Barrett had managed, despite all the financial scrimping, to save two quarters. So on Christmas morning, when the girls emptied their stockings, under the paper dolls their mother had cut out for them and under a couple of pieces of candy, they each found a coin.

Previous Christmas mornings had been more lavish, filled with frilly dresses and expensive toys. And there would be more such mornings in the future. But this was the Christmas the family would always remember.

In the future, even during the years of plenty, when the girls emptied their stockings, they always found— under the apples, oranges, nuts, and candy—a quarter.

It was a reminder—a reminder that some years are good while others aren't too good. Some years deliver new babies, promotions, raises, and great promises. Other years offer sickness, failure, death, and deep disappointment.

The quarter reminded them about both possibilities. It warned them not to write off all the pain of the past as if it didn't exist. It taught them that the sorrows and wounds of their lives had shaped their characters as much as their joys and accomplishments.

Anyone who takes seriously the Christmas stories of scripture knows that the first Christmas had more than angels, shepherds, wise men, and a mother nursing her baby. There was also the anguish of childbirth. There were the pungent, impolite odors of an animal pen. There was an old man who held the baby and told his mother, "A sword will pierce your own soul, too." There were the voices of many mothers screaming for their baby boys being slaughtered by a demented ruler named Herod. There was a breathless escape to Egypt.

The entrance of God's Son into the world meant peace—but it didn't assure that people would get along. It meant great joy—but it didn't mean we'd always get to grin. And it meant unconditional love—though it never implied that everyone would act lovingly.

And so one family, year after year, continued dropping a quarter of remembrance into the bottom of each child's stocking.

At least one of Channing Barrett's children picked up the tradition. Every year through the '30s, '40s and '50s, her five children, Dr. Barrett's grandchildren, pulled their stockings off the chimney on Christmas morning to find quarters buried under fruit, nuts, and candy.

And at least one of those five passed it on to her four children. And at least one of those four is passing it on to his three—no, his two—children.

The quarter has mysteriously tied this family together—binding even generations who have never met. Together they have remembered that bad year in 1918 and other bad years since.

One year brought the safe birth of a new nephew; another brought the self-inflicted death of a relative who couldn't keep fighting the demons of his life.

One year brought the thrilling news from the gynecologist that a baby was on the way; another brought the news from the pediatrician that the baby wasn't developing right.

Some years brought joy; others brought deep, deep pain.

The quarter is a remembrance that the meaning of Christmas is deeper than our triumphs and sorrows. It is a joy that can't fully be expressed, a peace that passes understanding.

For years my children have followed this tradition started by their Great Great Grandmother Barrett. Together, we've experienced the love of God, woven through the fabric of good days and dark days.

But never has the quarter meant more than today. There was one less stocking on the chimney in our home this morning. The death of Megan, our ten-year-old daughter, last month surely presents us with the darkest year of our lives. We now feel very connected to

Matthew's Christmas story, the one that tells of "Rachel weeping for her children."

But by God's grace we will survive. We're still together, we still love, we still hope, we still believe in that one who was born in Bethlehem. That's the message of our quarter this morning.

And even more, it's the message of Christmas.

Reprinted by permission of the author

Tumbleweed Smith of Big Spring is a popular West Texas radio celebrity, newspaper columnist, teacher, speaker, entertainer, and author. His website is tumbleweedsmith. com.

# The Big Stocking

by Tumbleweed Smith

Mary Urias of Fort Stockton has a beautiful family and a husband who loves her very much. He bought Mary her first bicycle after they were married. He gave her the first teddy bear she had ever owned.

Christmas is a big celebration around their house. Decorations are everywhere and Mary prepares a huge meal for everyone to enjoy in the midst of opening presents. Things now are quite different from the way they were when she was growing up in El Paso. She was one of nine children. Her mother was young and loved to party. Sometimes she would be gone over a three-day weekend and leave Mary to take care of the younger ones.

"I loved my mother," says Mary, "and I tried to be a good daughter. I did everything I could to make my mother love me. When she would leave, she would lock us in the house and tell us never to turn on the stove. She made us a big batch of oatmeal and put some canned milk in it. That's all we had to eat while she was gone: old gray, cold, hard oatmeal." Her mother often gave Mary whippings with a belt.

Santa Claus never came to Mary's house. The only present she got was from a grandmother who gave her a small sack that contained candy and nuts. Mary recalls one childhood Christmas: "I woke up very early. I jumped out of bed and started looking around. There was no Christmas tree. There was no Christmas dinner. There was no Christmas baking, no music, no nothing. It was just dark and gloomy in that little room.

"But I knew Santa Claus had come. I started looking everywhere to see what he had left me. My Mom told me I was not getting anything and told me to stop looking. But I kept looking. I looked everywhere, under pots and pans, in cabinets. The room was tiny but I searched everywhere. I looked out the window and knew that Santa Claus had come, because all the kids in the neighborhood had new clothes, shoes, they had skates and bikes. Little girls had little fur coats on. They had their buggies with their dolls. There were new puppies. There were toys. There was joy. And I didn't have anything. I went back to searching for my present from Santa Claus. I finally got on my mom's nerves. She pulled out that belt and gave me the whipping of my life."

One October when Mary was thirty-nine years old, she was in a restaurant with her daughter and husband and she told them this story. It was the first time they had heard it. A couple of months later, on Christmas day, Mary put her Christmas dinner in the oven, got her children dressed and went to church. When she got home, she rushed into her bedroom to change into comfortable clothes so she could put the finishing touches on her Christmas dinner. And there on the wall was a huge stocking nearly as tall as Mary. It was filled with presents and had a letter attached to it. The letter read: "Mary, for years I have been looking for you. I hope you can forgive me for being lost. I know we will have lots of good Christmases together. I'm glad I finally found you. I love you and I'm all yours. Your long-lost Christmas stocking."

Mary hangs that big stocking every year, right along with the stockings for her children and grandchildren.

Reprinted by permission of the author

*Jodie Wankowski says she is a West Texan in her heart, although she was born in Wisconsin and has lived in other states. An Air Force wife and mother, she fell in love with Texas during stints in San Angelo and Abilene, and she and her husband plan to retire in San Angelo. Her story was first published in the* San Angelo Standard-Times.

# A Little Something Extra

by Jodie Wankowski

An elderly couple who volunteered with me at an animal shelter told me this story.

One Christmas the husband planted a tree for the wife. It was her present. They were older empty nesters. She already had so many things.

During Christmas Eve night the husband planted the seedling. Wanting to make the gift extra special, he left something by it.

The next morning, he led his wife outside. Under the tree was a small striped kitten. Seeing the wife, the kitten uttered a sweet meow and ran over to her. The woman scooped up the creature and nuzzled its fur.

"Hank, I love it, thank you!" she squealed. "I never had a kitten and always wanted one!"

The trio soon became inseparable and, for years after, the woman declared the cat the best present ever. It was because of this cat's love that both became shelter volunteers.

The wife said the gift and Hank made that Christmas merry. I thought the story was heartwarming.

One day I was talking to Hank. "I sure hope my husband does something sweet for me this Christmas," I said, "just like you did for Helen all those years ago."

Hank smiled. "Don't worry," he said. "Sometimes sweet things just happen and Christmas has a way of making itself special."

"What do you mean?" I asked.

Again Hank smiled. "I planted the tree and put a gift certificate near it. The card was Helen's other surprise. The cat just showed up and made a present of himself. At that time, I hated cats, but when the wife's happy and thinking you're the greatest, you hold your peace. You can say the cat was a Christmas surprise for us both."

Reprinted by permission of the author

*James Bruce Frazier spent the early years of his life on the Cross Ell Ranch just west of Big Spring from 1927-1935. His book,* What I Learned on the Ranch, *closed with this story, a Frazier family favorite still told at Christmas, even after he died in 1989.*

# I Give You a Star

by James Bruce Frazier

There was so much land, so much sky, and few people to talk to. At night when it was dark, the sky spread all the way over us, beyond the Cross Ell Ranch, clear to where it touches the ground in every direction.

In school we read about interesting things, and when I came home there was no one to share them with, so I thought and thought about what I had learned. Some day I might get to tell people about it. I thought about some things they didn't teach me, but by putting them together I got new ideas.

In October we studied about Christopher Columbus, who discovered the New World—America. In was an exciting lesson, but it was not exactly a new discovery because there were people here before Columbus found it. He thought he was in India, so he called those people Indians.

Maybe they thought they had discovered Columbus, because neither of them knew about the other before October twelfth in 1492 when they discovered each other.

My teacher said Columbus sighted land and left his ship to come to the shore. When he got to the beach he spread his arms out wide and said in a loud voice, "I claim these lands for the queen!"

He set the flag and a Christian cross in the sand, and after that all the land was supposed to belong to Isabella of Spain, who probably never set foot on the lands he had given her in that little speech. Still, Spain owned a lot of new territory because of what Columbus said and did.

Well, I had a lot of time to think about that in the night time as I looked up into the Milky Way. That's the big strip of stars that reaches clear across the sky, and there are so many of them that I'll bet you never could count them all.

Looking up night after night, the thought came to me that nobody has ever claimed all those beautiful stars. I reasoned, "All the stars up there are free for the taking."

The more I thought about it the more I liked the idea of claiming them, all of them, hundreds and millions of them. They would all be mine, and I could do whatever I wanted with them because I'd be owner of the stars.

Columbus planted a flag when he claimed America, and I didn't know how to get a flag up there even if I had a flag. Then as I thought about it, it was almost like Sam, my on-duty guardian angel, whispered in my ear, "Son, you've got a flag. It's right up there in the sky just waiting for you to do something about it. See, it's the Cross Ell."

Sure enough, I could see a cross with a star off beside it in the shape of the Cross Ell cattle brand. I was so excited that I ran a little way out from the house where I could see all the sky everywhere. It made little shivers go down my back looking at it and thinking about what I was about to do.

I spread my arms and said in the biggest little-boy voice I could manage, "I claim all the stars in the sky as mine, mine, mine, by my right to unclaimed lands, and I take possession of it for God, my king. I own it, and there to prove it is our cattle brand, the Cross Ell, made out of stars for the world to see."

No one was listening unless it was Sam, and he didn't talk and no one ever saw him, so it was just like a secret. It was a secret I never forgot, and I'm telling it to you right now. I own all the stars in the sky, and I have for all the time since that wonderful night when I laid claim to them all.

I didn't claim the moon because that was too big and close, and I thought someone just might have claimed it before me, and I didn't want any arguments over ownership. I didn't claim the sun either, because to tell the truth I was so excited about owning all the stars I didn't even think about it in the dark. The sun was out of sight and out of mind when this great event took place.

Years have passed since I made my claim and to this day no one has disputed it, so I think maybe I really do own all the stars.

They fascinated me, and since I owned them, I figured I had better get to know them better, like riding over a new range to see what grew there. I found out that twinkling stars were really suns that may have planets circling them as our sun does. Then the planets probably have moons circling them, too.

Planets don't generate light but only reflect it, so you can't really see them from so far away, but Albert [another guardian angel] and Sam agree that they are really truly out there. Roscoe [daytime guardian angel] would say the same thing, only he was off duty about then.

I finally realized that no one really knows what all is included in my universe of stars, no more than Columbus and his queen knew what all was in the lands he claimed for Spain. He didn't know about the Mississippi River, the Grand Canyon, or even Texas. It was all there when he claimed it, and he didn't know it.

It was grand to be the owner of so vast a property. Then it was sad, because no one knew my secret. Such a wonderful thing has to be shared with others to bring full joy to the owner. I think that's the very reason God made mankind—to share the earth he had created, to bring full joy to God.

I know He owns the stars, I just laid claim to them as his servant, like Columbus claimed the New World for Queen Isabella.

Years passed and I have found owning all the stars is a lot more than one person can enjoy, so I thought about sharing them with others. I picked out one star in particular, where the Bar crosses the Ell in the cattle brand. That is my special star, and I shall keep it forever, even when I have passed on to where the buffalo and wooly mammoths have gone. That special star will be mine.

Now that I have chosen my own star, I'm setting about giving the rest of them away. I have so many I can give them to all nice people I meet and still have lots and lots of them left over. So I invite you to choose a star for yourself.

Now, when you pick one out, tell me where it is as I have told you how to locate mine. This way I shall always be able to look at your star and remember you, and you may do the same with mine. Our friendship will endure so long as those two stars shine in the midnight sky.

They will twinkle up there together when you and I are both gone from this earth. Folks who know this story will see our stars and remember we were everlasting friends.

This is the best use I can think of for the stars I have claimed. Remember it was a star that belonged to the Christ Child that brought kings and shepherds to the manger where he was born. Though I claimed the stars, I know they all belong to God, but for now I, like Columbus, have claimed them to put them to use in the cause of friendship.

You must go out into the star-filled night and choose your own. Take your time, mark it well, and tell me where it is, so you and I will always be together in the stars, no matter how far away we wander, one from the other. Take one of my stars as your special gift at Christmas, place its likeness on top of your Christmas tree, and remember the baby Jesus, then go outside in the night and look at our two stars, high in the sky.

That special star is yours forever. Help me give them all away to all your friends until every living person has his own friendship star, for as long as Christmas stars shall shine.

I'll do the same and think of you, while you think of me.

Reprinted by permission, McWhiney Foundation Press

*Albany rancher Bob Green was a historian and a great story-teller, as evidenced by this piece. He died in 2009.*

# A Shotgun and a Bird Dog

by Bob Green

Clyde was a good friend and neighbor of mine. I remember the Christmas day he discovered that trauma could take place as well as cheer on this usually happy occasion.

It had started out well. That morning under the Christmas tree, he had found a new, gas-operated automatic shotgun. It was the perfect Christmas gift for an avid quail hunter and he was eager to put it to use. As soon as the Christmas family feast was finished, he called his old faithful bird dog to join him and his son-in-law and they all piled into the flatbed pickup complete with wooden cattle sideboards.

The bird dog went into the back, and since old Tag sometimes got over-eager and would jump out prematurely, he was secured by a rope from his collar to a wooden standard inside the cattle racks.

So off went the happy hunters, son-in-law driving, down the gravel road, all three as happy as you could be on Christmas day.

Clyde was proudly handling his new shotgun, admiring it when suddenly a violent explosion left them wide-eyed and stunned, their ears ringing, the pickup cab filled with smoke and dust. Somehow the new shotgun had accidentally discharged, and since the barrel was fortunately pointed down, had blown a large, round hole in the pickup floorboard, through which the gravel road now appeared clearly—though looking startlingly out of place.

They stopped the truck, dismounted, and made a damage survey. Other than the hole in the floor, it appeared the pickup had escaped serious injury, so they loaded up once more and again headed for the awaiting quail, albeit somewhat subdued.

After a short distance, a grinding, clinking noise continuously filled the cab. "Oh, oh," Clyde said, "that sounds bad. I'm afraid that shot damaged this old pickup more than we thought."

So again they stopped and did a damage assessment. What they discovered did little for their already sagging morale. The Christmas shotgun's barrel had dropped down through the newly blasted hole in the floorboard and had been dragging along the gravel road. Their morale sagged even lower when, upon extricating the new gun, they observed that the end of the barrel had been ground away to about a 45-degree angle.

"My gosh," ruefully said Clyde, sadly gazing at the ground-off muzzle, "what else can happen?"

And then it happened. Old Tag, already excited by the events and seeing the two men standing outside with a gun, decided there must be quail nearby and in a climbing, leaping frenzy dove head first over the sideboards. Alas, the rope he was tied with was far too short for him to reach the ground, and he was jerked up short, tongue protruding, eyes bulging, all four legs stiffly extended, slowly revolving alongside the truck as he strangled.

With an anguished cry, Clyde sprang to the rescue. Placing his hands on the dog's rear, he began pushing Tag up and back over the sideboards. Just before clearing the top rail and dropping to safety inside the truck bed, one of Tag's frantically flailing hind legs, toenails extended, suddenly found secure lodging, unfortunately on Clyde's face. The toenails gouged bloody ruts from Clyde's eyebrows to chin before Tag dropped over into the back of the truck.

Unnerved by the horrible series of events, the two men looked at each other.

"Let's go home," Clyde finally said, mopping his bloody face with his bandana. "I've had about all the Christmas cheer I can stand for one day."

Reprinted by permission of Nancy Green

*Charlena Chandler, a native West Texan and retired teacher and librarian, is the author of* Not Far from Dryden, *a collection of newspaper columns she wrote, most of them for the* Odessa American. *This piece is from her book.*

# Giving Thanks for Small Gifts

by Charlena Chandler

Decades ago, some movie critics lambasted *The Sound of Music*—they said it was too clichéd, too sugary, too much. But audiences liked all that sweetness with children in lederhosen and dresses made of curtains and the movie went on to become one of the top moneymakers ever produced.

Let's recall some of Julie Andrews' favorite things. "Raindrops on roses and whiskers on kittens, bright copper kettles and warm woolen mittens."

I propose that many moments we love best in life are mundane—and that clichés are usually true. Small pleasures add to the great sum.

As a classroom exercise, I used to ask students to make list of things they were thankful for, as in favorite things, blessings if you will. They were asked to omit the natural inclusions, such as family, faith, country, and friends, which rightly belong but on another list, the for-granted list.

Think small, I said. Although I restricted them to ten choices, I'll break my own rules—rank has to have some privilege. Acknowledging that list-making in itself is rather clichéd, here's mine.

Hot homemade biscuits on a frosty winter morning, with butter and sorghum syrup, which I haven't been able to find in a while.

My hound Harriet sleeping in the sun. Bassets are cheerful dogs—don't let those soulful eyes fool you.

Riding around looking at Christmas lights.

The feel of rain in the air just before the first drops begin to fall.

The sound of little voices singing patriotic songs on July 4.

Full moons and star-filled summer nights in West Texas, far away from city lights.

Libraries and book stores. The very atmosphere of books.

Running water—creeks, rivers, streams, brooks.

Swarms of golden Monarch butterflies settling in the trees before they head south every fall.

Little boys playing with Legos, little girls with big bows in their hair.

Pecos River catfish. Fried, of course.

Receiving hand-written notes, mailed in an envelope with a stamp.

Newspapers. (Please don't remind me of their decline—I refuse to contemplate such a thought.)

The fragrance of sheets fresh from the clothesline.

High school marching bands. High school one-act plays.

Sitting around a campfire.

The music of the 1950s.

Drinking coffee in a China cup. Aunt Bertha said it tasted better and she was right.

Afternoon movies.

Mondays. Yes, that's strange. But last week is dead and gone and Monday offers a fresh beginning.

The old Broadway musicals—including *The Sound of Music*. I don't care what the critics said. Obviously, no one else did either.

Start your list now. It will make you think. And when dark winds blow, as they inevitably will, it will make you grateful for small reminders of sunlight.

Reprinted by permission of the author

It might be said that there are two kinds of people in the world: those who like fruitcake and those who hate fruitcake. The Abilene writer leaves little doubt where he stands on this controversial holiday issue.

# Don't Give Me a Fruitcake for Christmas

by Glenn Dromgoole

Don't give me a fruitcake for Christmas this fall. The last one you gave me I couldn't eat at all.

What are those green things and blue things and red? Are they still alive, or dormant, or dead?

I knew I couldn't eat it, right from the start, because of my liver—or kidney—or heart.

I didn't want to be seen as a jerk, so I just boxed it up and took it to work. No one would touch it and by the end of the day, not even the ants would take it away.

I offered slices to my former best friends. They haven't spoken a word to me since.

I fed it to the dogs and they turned up their noses and busted the fence and trampled the roses. I put it outside when they made such a fuss, and I wasn't surprised when it started to rust.

I tried it as a prop to hold open the door. It left a gooey spot on the hallway floor.

I put it on the end of a ten-foot pole, and dropped it to the bottom of a ten-foot hole, and poured in gasoline and threw in a torch. But the next day there it was, right back on my porch.

I finally gave it to my Aunt Ida Mary. (You probably noticed her obituary.) We buried it with her . . . and three days later—it showed up again in my refrigerator.

And there it has stayed for the rest of the year, gobbling my pickles and guzzling my beer, inhaling the whipped cream and butterscotch custard, the blackberry jelly and a new jar of mustard.

I'm stuck with it now, for worse, not for better. That's why I'm transcribing this urgent letter. I beg you: Don't give me a fruitcake this season. I'll refuse to accept it. I don't need a reason.

Reprinted by permission of the author

*Doug Mendenhall, journalist-in-residence and instructor at Abilene Christian University, writes a weekly column on spiritual matters for the* Abilene Reporter-News *religion page. Here, he has a little fun with the idea of how different Christians might decorate at Christmas.*

# Denominational Decorating

by Doug Mendenhall

Originally, the Rainbow Heights Neighborhood Association wanted to get everyone to agree to synchronize their holiday decorations—buy the same kind of lights, avoid gaudy inflatable Disney characters, that kind of thing.

Well, the problem is that once you get past the actual RHNA officers, the rest of the folks in the neighborhood don't like being told what to do by the ornament police. They want to express their individuality, not their conformity.

So anyway, the neighborhood association meeting had gone on for about three hours, and everyone was getting a little punchy even though it was virgin eggnog they were all drinking, and people started offering some pretty wacky alternatives to the original decoration regulations.

Next morning, nobody could believe the code that actually passed, but now Rainbow Heights is just stuck with it until next year.

The new regulations state that while nobody is required to decorate at all, every household that chooses to decorate for Christmas will do so according to their Christian denomination, as a way to express the unique personality of their faith heritage.

Here are a few samples of the new regulations:

Catholic: Multi-colored lights edging the house, but not so bright as to detract from the half-scale nativity scene, preferably with a spotlighted Mary touching or holding baby Jesus.

Episcopalian: No lights. Traditional decorations composed of greenery, red or gold ribbon, and real fruit.

Presbyterian: No lights except for white window candles. Most decorations composed of greenery, ribbon, and plastic fruit.

United Methodist: Exterior white lights only, but with window curtains thrown back to reveal a Christmas tree with red lights.

Lutheran: To highlight their German/Scandinavian background, blue lights edging the house and plastic candy canes edging the sidewalk, with window curtains thrown back to reveal a Christmas tree illuminated by real candles.

Southern Baptist: Multi-colored lights edging the house, the lawn, the trees, the mailbox, the trash cans, and any pets that linger too long in one spot.

Church of Christ: Only a small door wreath during the Christmas season. However, in April, lights may be placed on the house for about a month as a reminder that nobody really knows the exact date of Christ's birth.

Assembly of God: No more than 6,000 multi-colored tracer lights, six inflatable or plywood characters and six live animals at any one time.

Unitarian: One of every decoration mentioned above, but all placed in the back yard where they are less likely to offend others.

Now, this is obviously a contentious mess the RHNA has laid down, and I'm not sure it's going to work.

For one thing, what about all of the non-Christian families in the neighborhood? If most houses are showing off their faith by their decorations, then the non-decorating ones have to worry that people won't know whether they are abstaining because they are Muslim, Jewish, atheist, Sikh, Wiccan, or just too strapped to afford a bigger light bill.

I'm just not sure Rainbow Heights has thought this whole thing through. It may be that there is no way to regulate Christmas decorations and make everyone happy.

Or to regulate, organize, and constrain the celebration of Christmas in general.

I don't think Rainbow Heights can do it.

And I don't think the United States can do it.

And I don't think the world can do it.

But still and for all that, isn't it a glorious, lavish, multi-colored, multi-layered, multi-faceted celebration?

Whether yours is exquisitely tasteful or splashed with reckless abandon, may your soul be made merry by the thought that into this wide, wild, reckless world a single child is born, which is Christ, a savior for all.

Published by permission of the author

*David R. Davis of Fort Worth is an author, speaker, and cartoonist who has sixteen published picture books so far. His story is set on the Texas coast, certainly not in West Texas, but since the writer is from Fort Worth, "where the West begins," it seems appropriate to include it here. Besides, it's an awfully good story. The story is an excerpt from his e-book,* Travels with Grandpaw, *a memoir about growing up in Texas with his grandfather in the last century. For more information, visit his website at www.davidrdavis.com.*

# Wages for a Hired Hand

by David R. Davis

I loved spending the night at Grandpaw's house. He usually took me fishing somewhere, and I loved Grandmaw Lacy's cooking. She let me raid the plate of leftover biscuits, bacon, and cornbread she kept on the stove, and Grandmaw always had Cokes in her ice box.

She stocked the king-size Cokes, and I didn't have to half them with my brother or sister.

It was past dark when I heard Grandpaw's truck pulling up the driveway. The dogs barked while he put his paintbrushes, buckets, and ladders in the shed. I heard his shoes crunching on the gravel as he neared the house. He stomped his feet on the doormat, then the side door rattled open. Grandpaw looked like a whipped dog. He smelled of paint and kerosene.

"Lord, A'mighty, I'm give out," he said. "I'm about half froze, too. Sorry I'm late. I'm so blame hungry I could eat a dead mule's behind."

"Close the door, Raymond," Grandmaw said, "or we'll owe our soul to the gas company!"

Grandpaw shut the door and took off his white painter's cap. "I reckon I better get cleaned up," he said. I followed him down the hall to his bedroom.

His clean-up ritual never varied. First, he emptied his pockets on the bed and dumped his loose change into a coffee can in the closet. He laid out his clean khakis while Grandmaw drew him a bath. He took off his painting shoes and disappeared into the bathroom. The door cracked open a few inches.

"Here you go, Dave," he said. He tossed me his painter's clothes with a paint-speckled hand. "Give them to your Grandmaw. Be out directly." The door closed and

I heard him say "Ahhhhhhhh" as he settled into the hot water.

Grandmaw took the clothes straight to the washer and started a load. Just for fun, I sat down in Grandpaw's chair at the head of the table.

"You little heathen," Grandmaw said. "You know that's your Grandpaw's place!"

I retreated to my chair to the left of Grandpaw's. I watched as she sat all of the bowls and platters of food around his plate.

In a few minutes Grandpaw came in. He rubbed lanolin cream into his hands as he took his seat. He looked me over to make sure I'd combed my hair. "Dave, did you wash your hands?" he asked.

"Yes, sir," I said.

"Well, tuck in your shirt tail and bow your head."

I tucked in my shirt tail and bowed my head.

"Let's turn the thanks," Grandpaw said. He always started off in a strong voice, trailed off towards the end until the prayer was a whisper, but ended with a loud "Amen!"

"Heavenly Father," he said, "Accept our thanks for health, food, and lovin' kindness to us, and to all men. Amen."

Grandpaw filled his plate and started the food my way. "Help thyself," he said.

We got down to some serious working class eating, and then Grandpaw talked about his day. Aggravation colored his voice, as he speared a final piece of deer meat roast.

"Underwood showed up half drunk yesterday. He didn't show up at all today. Never hit the first sign of a lick. Had to finish the job by myself."

Grandpaw held out his cup.

"How about a little more coffee, Mother?"

Grandmaw poured him a cup and set it before him. He took a sip and sat the cup down on the red-checkered tablecloth. "I won't use him again," he said.

Grandpaw tilted his head towards me.

"Dave, when you take a job, show up on time. If you give the boss your word, keep it. Now, I ain't sayin' you have to take nothin' off nobody. If a boss jerks you around, tell him to go to hell, but if he's fair, give him a day's work for a day's pay. Folks want fellers they can count on."

Grandpaw's chair creaked as he leaned back. "A feller's word is the most important thing he's got. Ain't nothin' worse than a man whose word ain't no count."

After I helped Grandmaw clear the table, we watched an old Gary Cooper western on TV. After that, the Twelve Star Final News came on. After all the knife fights, car wrecks, and shootings, they showed a clip of Ike playing golf.

Grandpaw snorted.

"Well, there's another Republican on another golf course. When them boys get in, money always gets tight for the common man. They put their hands around the workingman's neck and squeeze. They never quite kill you; they leave you just enough air for you to barely make it."

I didn't know much about politics, but I'd heard Grandpaw's stories about hard times. Grandpaw blessed the memory of Franklin Delano Roosevelt, and he hated the Republican Party till the day he died. Grandpaw turned the TV off in disgust. "Mornin' comes early," he said. "Better turn in, Dave."

Grandmaw laid out sheets and one of her patchwork quilts on the couch for me. I stretched out in the dark thinking about how Grandpaw shoveled gravel during the Depression, daylight to dusk, for seventy-five cents a day.

Morning came too early for me. After breakfast, Grandpaw pulled on his jacket. "Dave, I got an errand to take care of before we go a'fishin.' Want to ride along?"

We climbed into his pickup truck and headed out Loop 13. After the engine warmed up, Grandpaw turned on the heater.

"Dave, that heater feels good. My toes was about froze."

"Where are we going, Grandpaw?"

"To Underwood's place to pay his wages."

This confused me.

"Grandpaw, how come you're paying Mr. Underwood? You said he didn't do any work."

Grandpaw didn't answer. After a few minutes we got to the San Antonio River Bridge. "Here's the cutoff to Underwood's place," he said.

We pulled off Loop 13 next to the river. A shack stood about fifty yards off the road next to a grove of pecan trees. Someone had knocked it together out of junk wood and tar paper. A tin stove pipe poked through a broken pane of glass on the side of the house. The December wind whipped the smoke around like a blue snake. Some dirty looking chickens pecked in the mud next to a junky looking car.

I noticed a kid about my age chopping kindling. He stared at me a moment and then went back to work. I could see his toes through a hole in one of his tennis shoes. I looked down at my new Keds and felt lucky.

Grandpaw turned his jacket collar up against the wind. "Dave, this will only take a minute."

We barely got the pickup door open before five little kids came running out of the shack. I couldn't believe all of them lived in that one room. None of them wore coats. Several had lines of snot running from their noses. One little kid only wore underpants.

"You kids better get inside out of this cold," Grandpaw hollered over the wind.

We walked up to the house.

A woman holding a small baby stood in the doorway. She wrapped the child in a blanket and stepped outside. I couldn't tell for sure how old she was. She must have been pretty young, but she had the face of an old woman. Her threadbare winter coat didn't match her faded print dress.

Grandpaw tipped his hat. "Good mornin', Mrs. Underwood. I brung your husband's wages."

"He ain't here, and I don't know where he is," she said, looking at the ground. "I didn't figure he had no wages a'comin', leastways none that he hadn't done drunk up."

Grandpaw pulled out his wallet. "Well, to be honest, Mrs. Underwood," Grandpaw said. "I come by a'hopin' he'd be gone." He opened the wallet and handed her several large bills.

"Here's his wages."

She stared at the bills.

"Thank you, Mr. Lacy," she whispered. It looked like tears in her eyes, but it could have been the wind. "I figured he done spent it."

"Now, Mrs. Underwood, you go straight to the store with that," Grandpaw said. "Don't you let him have it."

"He ain't gettin' a red cent!" she said. She shooed the kids inside. "You'uns get dressed. We're goin' shoppin'!"

Grandpaw tipped his hat again, and we got back in the truck. Mrs. Underwood still stood in the front yard, staring at the money in her fist. Grandpaw backed up and headed out Loop 13.

"Grandpaw, why'd you give Mrs. Underwood so much money? Yesterday, you said Mr. Underwood didn't have any wages coming."

Grandpaw rubbed his chin for a minute.

"Well, I thought about it a spell last night, Dave. Did you see them kids? She can't hardly keep 'em fed, and it's Christmas soon. Them young'uns want Santa Claus to come just like any other kid. It ain't their fault who their daddy is. Your Grandmaw might say what I done ain't good business, so keep it under your hat. The almighty dollar and all that. Now, let's stop by the barber shop and get our ears lowered before we head for the coast. The speckled trout will run up in the turn basins behind this cold front."

Grandpaw never mentioned what he'd done to anybody.

I grew up a little that morning. I realized, for the first time, that things aren't always black and white, and life isn't just a ledger book if you live it right. Sometimes a man has to dispense a little grace if he's to be a real human being.

Reprinted by permission of the author

*Reba Cross Seals of Alpine enjoys writing, teaching, and painting in the mountains of West Texas. She is president of Texas Mountain Trail Writers, which sponsors an annual writing conference (texasmountaintrailwriters.org).*

# The Nomad Princess Christmas

by Reba Cross Seals

The Nomad Princess leaned back against the rough gray upholstery of the back seat of the dark green 1941 Ford. It was Christmas Eve, 1948, and the Nomad Princess had been riding for several hours crowded up with her lowly handmaiden, Lady Ruth, while boxes unevenly were stacked at their feet, and books slid between them. The homemade two-wheeled trailer bounced grumpily along behind the car, carrying all the family's worldly possessions, leaving the farm far behind.

Irritation at having to be a Princess cramped up in an old Ford, moving yet once again, to wherever Daddy's oil company surveying job happened to take them, was just about more than the Princess could take. Lowly Lady Ruth read her book and ignored her sister, the Princess, except to complain when the Princess' loud sighing threatened the peace of the Christmas Eve journey.

It wasn't yet dusk when Daddy first announced from the front seat, "Hey, girls, listen! The radio just said that Santa and the reindeer have just been sighted over Canada! It won't be long now!" Then Daddy proceeded to announce hourly bulletins: "Now he's entered the United States! I wonder if he can feel the temperature increase." And later: "Now he's over Colorado. Hope he doesn't strike any reindeer hooves on Pike's Peak!"

And much later when the only light was the eerie glow from the radio dial and car lights meeting us on the narrow two-lane roads, "Santa's over Arizona now! Wonder what he thinks about that Grand Canyon!"

And much, much later: "Reba and Ruth, guess what! He's over Texas now! He just crossed over that barbed wire fence between Amarillo and the North Pole! Don't give up now! He's almost here." (Daddy never did understand that he had a Nomad Princess in the car.)

During all those cheerful announcements, Mother smiled tiredly at her two girls, passed out homemade sandwiches, and quietly tried to figure how they were going to cram her family of four into the only house her husband had been able to rent in the new town, a small one bedroom. She and her husband both had a hard time adjusting to the nomadic life of oil exploration companies after the farm life they had been forced to leave behind. She hoped Hoyt had remembered to pack the box with the new dolls near the door of the trailer so that they could be found tonight on Christmas Eve.

The Nomad Princess was worrying, and had been since the announcement of the latest move by the seismograph crew. She worried a lot more than the cheerful Lowly Lady Ruth, her handmaiden. How on earth would Santa be able to find them tonight when they were on a dark lonely highway going to a town she never heard of? Santa probably hadn't either. She sighed again, fiercely biting her lip to keep back tears. It would never do for her handmaiden to see her crying. So she pinched her instead.

With head bouncing against the window as sleep fought worry for her attention, she again heard Daddy announcing, "He's just cleared Abilene, coming our way! Faster, too, cause his sleigh is lighter with all the presents that he's dropped off along the way." As the Nomad Princess' eyes snapped open, her heart dropped to her oxford clad toes. No way could he find them now. They had passed through miles and miles of a tall pine forest, crossed innumerable rackety-clackety wooden single-lane bridges, and went through little towns that weren't even large enough to merit a name sign on the highway.

The Nomad Princess barely woke when Daddy finally opened the back car doors, carried sleeping Lowly Lady Ruth up the steps into the room at a small tourist court, and Mother half walked, half carried the Princess in behind them. The girls tumbled together into a bed, so weary that the Nomad Princess' last thought was, "Never mind, maybe Santa will find us next Christmas." Only a few tears rolled onto the strange pillow before she was fast asleep.

❄ ❄ ❄

A few weeks later Mother and Daddy were visiting with friends on their seismograph crew who had moved with them, as the adults played their monthly 42 domino game. The visitors' three little girls were playing with the beautiful new dolls that the Movie-Star Queen and her Wardrobe Assistant Ruth had received from Santa.

Mother passed around coffee with her special buttermilk pie, and said to her friends over the Formica dinette table, "Well, you're lucky that your children were with their grandparents during the move. It was really difficult for us having to move on Christmas Eve, especially with Santa Claus and all. But, thankfully, our kids are so young that, actually, I don't think that they noticed any problem at all."

Published by permission of the author

*Carlton Stowers, a native West Texan, is the author of more than forty books and recipient of the A. C. Greene Award given to a distinguished Texas author. This story first appeared in* American Way Magazine *published by American Airlines.*

# Christmas Comfort

by Carlton Stowers

He was broke, both financially and in spirit, as that long ago holiday season approached. The father and his two young sons had moved to a rural setting, there to rebuild their lives in the wake of divorce; they by meeting new friends and tasting new country boy adventures, him struggling to carve out a living as a self-employed writer who had left behind a newspaper career.

The kids had been far more successful with the transition, oblivious to such realities that if an overdue payment didn't soon arrive from some publisher, tending the rent on the small stone cabin they called home might pose a problem.

Such was not their worry to suffer. Ages five and eight, theirs were days of warm innocence with no concern more serious than whether the fish would be biting along nearby Cypress Creek when the school bus delivered them home.

As the Christmas season arrived, their new home, a little community called Comfort, began to sparkle with the colored lights strung along the eves of houses. The man and his boys followed the tradition of most of their neighbors, locating a small, well-shaped cedar sapling on a nearby hillside and taking it home for decorating.

There was the annual holiday band concert in the high school auditorium, a moonlit night of church-sponsored caroling through the town, and while there was no snow, a sudden ice storm briefly turned the landscape into a winter wonderland. And there was the steady adult hum of excited whispers about gifts bought, wrapped, and hidden away.

Yet as the days too quickly passed, the man struggled with little success to find joy in the season. With the postman arriving empty-handed day after day, he worried that his first Christmas as a single father would be remembered for what it was not rather than for what he'd hoped it would be.

He had shopped carefully, his limited funds spent on small items—a puzzle book here, a toy or two there, wrapping paper, and a spool of red ribbon—in hopes that once they were placed beneath the tree they would appear as more than they really were.

One evening, long after his sons were sleeping, the man sat alone in a room illuminated only by the single string of lights on the tree, pondering the meager offering of gifts. *Christmas was not just about an abundance of toys and trinkets, right? Hadn't we, as a generation, over-indulged our kids?*

So deeply in thought was he that he didn't hear the first few late night rings of the phone. When he finally answered, he heard the cheerful voice of his sister. She and her husband were thinking about making a drive through the picturesque Texas Hill Country. Okay if they stopped in for a visit?

The man had not seen them since the move and his gloom was swept away by the prospect of their coming. That in itself would be a welcomed gift.

By the time they arrived the house had been cleaned spotless, the giddy anticipation of guests warming the day. The aroma of freshly brewed coffee wafted through the kitchen.

They hugged, talked, and laughed for some time before the brother-in-law suggested that his wife would enjoy a tour of the town. She wanted to see the boys' school, where their friends lived, view the landscape of their new life. And so they soon departed, leaving only her husband behind to rest from his long drive.

It was a few hours before they returned to find him asleep on the couch. In the corner where the Christmas tree stood, gifts in a rainbow of colored wrappings were piled. Large and small, they formed a dazzling display. Additional lights and new ornaments had been added to the tree and a tiny angel smiled down from the top of its branches.

In the years that followed, the writer-father would forge a new life, a modest degree of prosperity ultimately achieved. He is old now, his sons long since grown to manhood. Yet each year when a new chill invades the air and the holiday season approaches, he thinks back to that special time and an unexpected act of loving kindness.

To this day it is the fondest of my Christmas memories.

Reprinted by permission of the author

*San Angelo novelist Elmer Kelton, voted by his fellow Western writers as the greatest Western author of all time, wrote mostly historical fiction set in Texas. But he also published several works of nonfiction, including a book of Christmas stories,* Christmas at the Ranch, *from which this is excerpted.*

# Christmas at the Ranch

by Elmer Kelton

Dad never looked forward to Christmas with quite the excited anticipation of us kids. For one thing, livestock did not recognize the holiday. They needed just as much attention on Christmas as on the days before and after.

Christmas was a distraction that broke into the ranch's orderly routine. The cowboys usually liked to take a few days off to go back to their own homes and celebrate with their kin, an understandable if disruptive desire. It was left to Dad to carry the full load while they were gone. He would never spend more than one night away from home, and seldom even that.

Mother saw Christmas in a more traditional happy light. She had grown up in an Oklahoma farming and ranching home where Christmas meant a trip to church, family singing of hymns and carols, and a tree with all the trimmings, mostly homemade.

Dad had grown up in a spartan ranch atmosphere more than twenty miles north of Midland, Texas, in a time when a wagon trip to town and back took two days. His family lived far from church or organized Christmas activity. There was no Christmas tree, not even a forlorn local cedar, for a treeless open prairie lay all around. In later years that country would produce a serious infestation of mesquite, but during Dad's boyhood a chuck-wagon cook would travel far out of his way to pick up what scant firewood he could for the next camp.

It was customary for schools and churches to set up community-type trees, but a family tree in the home was rare. It took years for Dad to reconcile himself to the notion of bringing a tree into the house. To him it was as out of place as a horse or cow would have been. Eventually he softened to the idea of chopping down a medium-sized cedar tree on the south end of the ranch where they flourished and setting it up in the living room. He was conscious of the fire hazard, for a dry cedar could easily explode into flame. Fortunately ours never did. Nobody ever lighted real candles on it.

Mother recalled an incident early in my parents' marriage that might have had a bearing on Dad's ambivalent attitude about Christmas. Florey was a small community, now almost forgotten, near Andrews, Texas. The church there had a Christmas Eve celebration with a tree and presents.

Mother's two youngest sisters, Ruth and Christine, were small girls at the time. Dad entered the church ahead of the rest of the family, carrying two Christmas-wrapped dolls under his coat. As he started to place them under the tree, one of them cried, "Mama!"

The crowd laughed. Red-faced, Dad retreated to the back of the church. For years afterward he avoided both churches and Christmas trees.

In his later years, when his grandchildren were small and enthusiastically awaiting Santa Claus, he yielded to the Christmas spirit and enjoyed it as much as they did.

Reprinted by permission, McWhiney Foundation Press

*Natalie Bright, author of* Oil People, *is a free-lance writer, office manager and mom and is married to a geologist and rancher. She grew up in Dimmitt, now lives in Canyon. Her website is nataliebright.com.*

# A Cowboy's Christmas Blessings

by Natalie Bright

Jeremy watched the steam rise from his hot chocolate as he plopped five marshmallows into the mug. He stirred and stirred and then brought a spoonful of the sweet brown liquid to his lips.

Glancing out the picture window, the sight of their ranch foreman caught his eye. Cecil stood on his front porch across the road. The cowboy waved at Jeremy and turned up his collar against the December cold. His jeans were tucked into tall boots and a red wild rag peeked from the neck of his barn coat. He tugged his black lid further down on a grey head and sauntered toward the barn. Two excited cow dogs, one blue and the other red, circled and hopped around his legs.

"Mom," said Jeremy. "Why doesn't Cecil have a Christmas tree in his house?"

"I guess he quit putting one up after Miss Lola died. This will be his second December without her," she said.

Jeremy looked at the beautiful evergreen towering to the vaulted ceiling in their family den before turning up the mug and waiting for the final drip to land on his tongue.

"I'd like some, please." Little sister, Kaylee, clambered up into the bar stool next to her big brother.

Jeremy frowned. "Everybody should have a tree. It's Christmas Eve."

He hopped down, yanked on his cowhide boots and his heavy field coat. After squeezing his head into a blue knitted cap, he dug work gloves out of his pocket.

Kaylee spun around on her stool, forgetting all about her request, and asked, "Where you going?"

"I'm busy," said Jeremy.

"Doing what?" She dashed over to the mudroom wall and jerked her jacket down off of the hook.

"I've got working chores to do," said Jeremy. "Serious stuff."

Kaylee pulled her hood over her head. "I'm going with you."

Now on any normal day, Jeremy would tell her no and order her to leave him alone, and then Kaylee would run from the room sobbing with all of the drama she could muster. But on Christmas Eve he thought twice about making his little sister cry.

So he said nothing and stepped out into the cold blast of winter air. The tip of his nose tingled as he walked towards the barn. Kaylee fell into step behind him.

"Hey, Cecil," called Jeremy. He walked into the sweet smell of hay and horses.

"Over here," was the reply. They found him filling a feed bin in one of the stalls for Brick, his roan gelding. Jeremy balanced on the fence rail. Puffs of warm breath blew from the horses' nostrils and drifted into his face.

"I got a question." He paused, trying to figure out how to voice the words he wanted to ask. Kaylee squeezed through the slats and patted Brick's neck.

"Out with it boy," Cecil said. "I can tell something's buggin' you. What is it?"

"I was wondering why you don't have a Christmas tree?"

"Don't need one," said Cecil.

"Have you seen ours? We have lots and lots of lights and I made the paper chain," said Kaylee. "Don't you like any of that stuff?"

Cecil looked over Brick and rested his arms across the horse's back.

"Every night I look up at the big Texas sky where I see a billion stars shining like all get out. Those lights overhead spread from horizon to horizon and twinkle prettier than anything I've ever seen on a fake evergreen."

"What about presents?" said Jeremy. "You don't have any place to put your presents."

"Well sir, when I roll out of bed in the morning my present is being able to see another sunrise. There's 'bout near every shade I could imagine on the horizon with more colors than any decoration you could buy in a store. I hate to miss even one morning of God's glory."

"What about family?" said Jeremy. "You never have anyone come visit you on the holiday."

"Don't need 'em," said Cecil. "Got no time to be lonely. When I walk out to the barn, Brick and the horses are waiting to greet me. We've got the dogs and the other ranch critters. Plus I've got you and Kaylee, and your mom and dad. At round-up and branding this whole place is covered with friendly West Texas neighbors willing to lend a hand. My grandfather and father worked at this ranch and I've been riding for the brand my whole life. There's no place I'd rather be." said Cecil.

"Our choir sings carols at the hospital. Maybe I should ask my teacher if we could sing for you," offered Kaylee.

"He's not sick," said Jeremy.

"I've got me carolers all year long," said Cecil. "Every evening the coyotes serenade me as I sit on the porch drinking my coffee, and in the spring the meadowlarks and barn swallows chirp their good mornings. When the wind stirs up those cottonwoods over yonder into a rustling racket, the noise they make is just as sweet as any holiday music I've ever heard."

"Look! It's snowing," Kaylee pointed and Jeremy ran to the entrance of the barn. Flecks swooped and swirled in the slant of light. The wind whispered a promise of more on its way.

Cecil joined them at the door. "There is one thing. I sure do miss the smell of Lola's pumpkin bread. There's nothing I've found even close to that."

They watched the flakes dance and dart against a graying sky. Silent, random specks soon turned into a frenzy of blowing white.

"I guess you could say I'm a lucky man," said Cecil. "It's Christmas all year long at my house."

"Do you have any hot chocolate?" asked Jeremy.

"With marshmallows?" Kaylee blew air into her beet red fingers and hopped from one leg to the other.

Cecil thought for a minute. Kind blue eyes twinkled under pale bushy eyebrows as his weathered face broke into a wide grin.

"Nope," he said. "That's where you kids got me."

"I'm telling Momma about the Christmas lights that stay on in the sky," Kaylee said over her shoulder as she ran into the curtain of snow.

Jeremy tugged his cap over his aching ears. The dogs lay at his feet while he and Cecil watched the storm for several minutes. Jeremy broke the silence. "So when I wake up in the morning on Christmas Day, it can be like that day over and over again?"

"That's the way I see it," said Cecil.

The taste of cocoa still lingered on Jeremy's lips which reminded him how cold his nose felt. "Want some hot chocolate?"

"That would be good," the old cowboy said. "Lead the way."

With hunched shoulders and chins tucked into turned up collars, two cowboys stepped out into the storm and into another year of blessings.

Published by permission of the author

Don Knecht of Abilene, a longtime Boy Scout executive, recalled a special Christmas in 1944 on the front lines of World War II. He died in 2002.

# Christmas at War

by Don Knecht

On Christmas Eve 1944, some of the thoughts of this member of the 71st Infantry Regiment turned homeward as we occupied a desolate French farm about six miles from the German border.

We were less than a hundred miles from the German town my great-grandfather left to come to America in 1854. My dad had entered combat in World War I less than seventy-five miles from this farm.

A long line of half-frozen infantrymen plodded silently by us headed in the direction we had come. I asked one where they were going and he mumbled he thought it was Belgium. Two divisions on our front were being sent to the critical Battle of the Bulge to the north-west of us.

In spite of the fact that there was now nothing between us and the Germans, this was Christmas Eve and one of our men found a cedar tree and a box of decorations. We put it up in a hay barn and ate our C rations.

Then orders came to move to a new position. The last thing we loaded was the Christmas tree, still decorated.

Our truck must have been quite a sight pulling a 57mm anti-tank gun behind, a 50-caliber machine gun mounted on top of the cab, and the gun crew sitting in the back with the Christmas tree standing erect in the middle.

It was just as well that we did not know that the Germans would capture that gun in a New Year's Day attack, a week later. But for a little while, as we rode through the frozen countryside on Christmas Eve night, our Christmas tree helped to bring our thoughts and memories closer to home.

Reprinted by permission of Josie Knecht

*This story by longtime columnist Rick Smith ran in the* San Angelo Standard-Times *on Christmas Day, 2012.*

# Christmas in Jail
by Rick Smith

It's not a place anyone would choose to spend Christmas.

We make our way to the second floor of the Tom Green County Jail, then follow a guard to a big, bare room. Dark gray paint covers the cold, concrete block walls. A toilet in the corner of the room is only partially screened. What looks like a concrete floor completes the bleakness.

About the size of a racquetball court, the room is at least twenty feet high. The terrible acoustics send sounds ricocheting off the building's metal walls and bouncing down the endless hallways.

The room's heavy metal doors and shielded observation windows are a reminder the room wasn't built to lock people out. It's to keep inmates in.

A small group from the Diocese of San Angelo brings in a movable Mass, complete with guitar and songs and hope.

A man carefully washes the top of a small table. He covers it with a snow-white cloth and lights two candles. The man places a large red Bible and a beautiful golden cup—a chalice—on the table. The polished chalice gleams.

A woman tunes her guitar, strums, begins to sing. Two more women join her, then two more. The first verse of "Go Tell It on the Mountain" floats to the high ceiling.

A guard leads a line of nine female inmates into the room. They wear jail-issue baggy orange blouses and pants. On their feet are slippers or flip-flops.

They are not shackled or handcuffed. The women don't look dangerous. They look tired and form two lines in front of the table as the bishop enters.

The Most Rev. Michael D. Pfeifer, of the Catholic Diocese of San Angelo, has served the area as bishop since 1985. He carefully slips into a brilliantly white robe and a bishop's tall hat as the choir sings "O Come All Ye Faithful."

"May the peace of God be with you," he begins. "Good morning. Buenas dias!"

The bishop has held jail Masses for almost thirty years. He began while a priest in San Antonio and said it felt like something he "should do at Christmastime." There are people in jail who cannot go to church or see their families, he explained. Instead, church and families must go to the jail.

The Christmas Eve Mass seems to pass quickly.

"Sometimes we fail," he tells us. But, he adds, "God is very merciful."

He reads the Christmas story, the birth of Jesus, from the Bible's Gospel of Luke, then explains its importance in words all can understand. His words instruct and comfort and give hope.

He asks where the women would choose to be on Christmas Day.

"Home," they say, one after another.

He prays and urges inmates to offer their own prayers. Several do. The choir sings "Angels We Have Heard on High."

Holy Communion is followed by hugs as the women turn to one another, some in tears.

The bishop visits with the prisoners, one by one, speaking softly as the choir sings "Silent Night," then "Joy To the World," then "We Wish You a Merry Christmas."

By the time the choir begins its last song, "Feliz Navidad," everyone's clapping along. Some of the inmates join the singing.

The joyful message flows out of the room. Floating past locked doors and barred windows and cold metal.

Reprinted by permission, *San Angelo Standard-Times*

*This story by Betty Davis, Abilene writer, civic leader, and former school board president, first ran as a guest column in the* Abilene Reporter-News.

# A Coat for Christmas
by Betty Davis

Growing up, I never had a coat that was *originally* mine. It's not like I was ever cold. Who could be cold when there are a plethora of cousins to share clothes? However, I knew at about age thirteen that I needed my *own* coat when I spotted one displayed in a store window.

I had plenty of clothes, just never store bought. My mother made my clothes, sometimes making a dress from one of hers. She took care of me, plain and simple. But this time, I wanted a coat that smelled, not like a cousin, but like a store, with tags still attached. I probably didn't say much, though I was sure that this was the Year of the Coat.

A week before Christmas, a coat-sized box was tucked under the tree and my mother beamed. I beamed. There was a secret and both of us knew it!

We always opened presents on Christmas Eve, yet this year when my grandmother came to visit, Mother asked if I wanted to open my present a day early. She couldn't wait to see my surprise, and neither could I!

I unwrapped the present slowly to savor the moment, while my grandmother and mother held their breaths. I knew I'd never forget this moment and I never have.

I lifted the box top and . . . there was a doll . . . my old doll . . . surrounded by new doll clothes. My heart sank, followed by my face. I looked at my mother and her heart, her face, mirrored mine. For a moment, we stared at one another as the truths sunk in.

We didn't have much money. My mother and grandmother had spent hours making a beautiful wardrobe for a doll that they hadn't noticed I'd outgrown. Beautifully made, beautifully packaged, beautifully given.

I tried, really tried, to act excited. It was too late. My mother saw my disappointment, my embarrassment. I saw her disappointment, her embarrassment. Both of us cried. I'd already lost the desire to play with dolls. Now I'd lost the desire for a new coat.

Some Christmases later, my sister told me that my husband had gotten me a coat for Christmas. I didn't want a coat, I wanted a watch. I'd never had a watch. She warned me to look surprised and happy come Christmas morning. He was so proud.

Remember the mouton coats that were the rage for a couple of years, then avoided like the flu? She said he'd bought a mouton; it was on sale. (Where would they even be on sale?) The more she talked about his excitement and how I was to be excited, the madder I got—at him, for buying the dumb thing, and at her, for not telling him. After all, he was a teen-ager with no clue about style! I didn't have a clue either but I knew about moutons, and so did she!

I stewed for two weeks while she raved on.

Sure enough, a coat-sized box was tucked under my sister's tree. He beamed, she smiled. I looked away.

Christmas morning came and, with dread, I slowly unwrapped the box. I lifted the box-top and . . . no coat! Only another small, sweetly wrapped box. The little box held a beautiful pear-shaped watch with a diamond so tiny you couldn't see it. That didn't matter; both of us knew it was there.

My sister was most pleased with herself. She, her husband, and mine, laughed at my expense all day; they thought they were so clever. I didn't care, I was both excited and relieved—excited about my watch, relieved about the coat.

Since that long-ago time, I've had countless coats and jackets—every weight, style and length—many I've forgotten. But my favorite Christmas coat stories, the ones I savor, are the two Christmases when I didn't get a coat at all.

Reprinted by permission of the author

*Frank Grimes, legendary editor of the* Abilene Reporter-News *from 1919-1960, wrote a number of Christmas editorials for the newspaper over the years, many of which were collected in a book,* Lone Star Christmas, *edited by Dr. Charles Marler in 1989. This is one of the pieces from that book.*

# A Coconut for Christmas

by Frank Grimes

We don't know if this is a proper Christmas story or not, but we have been wanting to tell it for a long time—and if it isn't exactly factual, it isn't fictional either, but a compound of both. For what is truth except the essence that is distilled out of a man's memory of things experienced, things seen and felt, things heard, things dreamed of and wished for—even things feared and derided. Some people say Santa Claus is an arrant old fraud himself, but we know better than that. So you'll have to make up your own mind whether it's truth or fiction, for after almost fifty years we are a bit confused about some of the details ourself.

There came into our little Central Texas community set in a cove of the calcareous hills a man and his wife and their son Walter. It's odd, but Walter's is the only name we recall. They were obviously of ancient peasant stock from somewhere between the Elbe and the Oder. Poppa looked old and beat-up at forty, bent with toil, his arms swinging down to his knees—the very caricature of a man; even his walk was like that of an ape, a sort of swinging lurch, from long stooping in the fields. Momma still wore the outlandish clothes she landed in, and continued to do so for years, for this was a very poor family. Walter was a towhead and as quiet and subdued as his parents.

After a year or two of working for other farmers, Poppa bought the scrawniest, most run-down farm in the neighborhood, almost as much rock as soil, and people criticized the vendor for taking a foreigner shamelessly in.

But Poppa worked morning, noon, and night, moving rocks from the field and building from them fences, a barn, a cowshed, and finally a house half as big as the barn, which seemed to be the custom of his people.

Pretty soon the little farm was yielding a living of sorts and people became accustomed to the odd foreigners when they came to town in the family wagon. Momma would bring in butter and eggs to swap for staples, and Poppa occasionally planked down a few small coins for an axe handle or a pound or two of nails. Walter always tagged along behind his Momma, who always tagged along three paces behind Poppa, for that too was a custom of their country.

The young idlers of the town usually had something cute to say to the trio, though of course they did not understand the language. It was the smart thing to do to say something nasty in a pleasant tone of voice, for the strangers would smile and nod as though they had been complimented. Only one boy refrained from this form of ridicule—Joey, the charcoal burner's son, who spent most of his nights hunting coons and possums in the coves and on the ridges with his dog Samson. Joey would walk away in disgust when the raillery started. Once he had been the object of this sort of ribbing, but only once; he had gone at the ribber in a fury of flying fists and that was that.

Well, just before one Christmas—it was the time of the panic in '07 [1907]—the foreigners came to town and Poppa pulled his team into a vacant lot, dropped the outside traces, wrapped the lines around a standard, and they all got down. They strolled up the main business "street" like three waddling ducks—Poppa, Momma and

Walter as always, Poppa in front, Momma in the middle, and Walter behind.

Momma went into the general store with her basket of eggs and butter. Poppa went to the hardware emporium, and Walter, eyes a-bug, drank in the few Christmas goods and decorations visible along the street.

Our gang was in rare good form, and started to pester Walter, who said nothing. Joey went off around the corner with a frown of distaste on his face.

Minutes later here came Poppa from the hardware store with a hand held behind his back, and Momma from the grocery with a few skimpy purchases in her apron. They met where Walter was absorbed in a Christmas display.

Poppa tapped Walter on the shoulder and the youngster whirled. Poppa brought his hand out from behind his back and displayed a huge coconut with the husk still on.

"Look, Valtar!" he cried, his face split in a rare smile. "Coocoonut! Coom, Valtar, we go home. What you say, Chris'mas now, eh! Coom, Valtar—Coocoonut!"

Walter danced in glee, his face shining. And so they set off toward their wagon—Poppa marching proudly ahead, Momma coming next, and Walter dancing around them. Momma's care-worn face was wreathed in a smile that glowed, and there was happiness and pride in her eyes. It was the first time we learned joy could transfigure an ugly face into a beautiful one.

We all laughed out loud, of course; it was so funny. For years "Com, Valtar, coocoonut" was good for a laugh anytime. (How were we to know that industry and frugality and faith could work such miracles? How could we know that in time the little house would grow and become a big one, and that Walter would become a noted surgeon?)

Well, anyway, about that time Joey came around one corner and that tattletale, pigtailed brat of a sister of his came around the other corner, and the little stinker screamed: "Joey's got a coconut and he won't give me any! The old stingygut!"

Joey was furious. "Shut your mouth, you little fool! I ain't got no coconut neither! You mind your own business."

Well, we got a good laugh out of that too, but not out loud, knowing Joey. And it took this writer about six months to figure out what Joey had done with his coconut.

Reprinted by permission, ACU Press

*From 1987-1992 Jack Boyd wrote a weekly short story set in the fictional town of Cedar Gap, south of Abilene, for the Saturday edition of the* Abilene Reporter-News. *Three collections of the stories were published by Texas Tech University Press, and he also has a Christmas collection available on CD, which includes this story. For more information, see his website, cedargapbooks.com.*

# A Corn Shuck Christmas

by Jack Boyd

Well, for the Saturday before Christmas, it's a lot quieter here in Cedar Gap then we expected. Oh, our little **Christmas parade was a big success, and the town Christmas tree is glittering more than usual. But for the four Gallart kids it's a time of quiet reflection and hushed stock taking.**

Joe Tom Gallart is twelve and Cookie is six. Eva and Max are in between. The four have stayed with foster parents when a family could be found that would put up with them, but the placement never lasted more than two or three weeks. The kids considered the foster home a game, a challenge, to see how fast they could be thrown out.

Yesterday it was Deputy Sheriff Donnie Sue Kingsbury's turn to get them a place until the state's bureaucracy could kick in.

"I need somebody with the self-control to keep from killing those kids." Donnie Sue frowned at the Palace Cafe crowd. "Anybody available for a couple of days?"

The Gallart kids' reputation had preceded them. Listeners found a profound need to study their coffee grounds or peer at the traffic outside.

"I think I can take them for a few days."

Heads came up, eyes squinted. The soft voice belonged to CoraMarie Minson, the kindest, gentlest soul in Cedar Gap.

Donnie Sue frowned. "I dunno, CoraMarie. Those kids are kinda frisky."

CoraMarie wrinkled her nose. "Pshaw! They're kids. You've just got to treat them a bit differently." She set her cup firmly on the table. "I may be 75, but I'm not dead. I'll take them."

Donnie Sue waited, then sighed. "OK, I'll bring 'em over this afternoon."

Promptly at 3:00, Donnie Sue herded the four wary, smirking Gallart children into CoraMarie's living room. After the introductions CoraMarie smiled and said, "I'm very pleased to have you, Joe Tom and Eva and Max and Cookie. I've been needing someone to help me finish a project for some children I know."

The four glanced at each other. "Nobody said anything about work," Joe Tom mumbled. "We don't work."

"Oh, this isn't actually work," CoraMarie said quietly. Her shy smile and tiny voice caught the four children off guard. "It's more like play."

Eva straightened, her eyes mistrustful. "What kinda play?"

"I need you to help me make some dolls."

Joe Tom, his street smarts sensing a patsy of monumental proportions, shook his head. "No work. We don't have to. We just want supper."

"And you'll get it, right after we gather the material for the dolls," CoraMarie said softly. "We just need a few ears of corn with the shucks still on."

Joe Tom saw he was outflanked. He frowned, then nodded curtly, and the four children followed CoraMarie into her back yard garden. She showed them how to pull the shucks just right so they came off in one piece.

Back in the house CoraMarie pointed to four chairs around her kitchen table. She picked up an ear of corn, broke it cleanly, then handed it to Eva. "Here, Eva, you look like you understand dolls. Just do what I do and we'll have some fine gift dolls."

Eva's eyelids lowered. "I don't give dolls away. I'm gonna keep mine."

CoraMarie nodded. "Maybe we can work it so you can get the dolls back later."

"You mean," Eva said slowly, "they'll take the dolls away from the kids?"

"No. The children won't need them anymore."

Joe Tom leaned forward. "Why won't they need the dolls?"

"Because the children will be dead. Now, here's how we're going to make the hair for the dolls."

Joe Tom swallowed, his eyes wide and frightened. "Whatta ya mean, dead? This some kinda joke?"

"No," CoraMarie said. She took a deep breath. "These are some children in a home that have bad diseases, and the doctors can't cure them. So they're going to die. These little dolls will give them something pretty to play with. And knowing they came from other children should make them feel better, don't you think?" She peered deeply into each child's eyes.

The three youngest looked at Joe Tom, but he'd never run into this kind of problem before. His own lack of love and understanding had prevented his ever acknowledging another human's need. Here he finally found a situation that was worse than his own. He had no answer for CoraMarie Minson's soft voice.

With a tremor like a severe chill, Joe Tom picked up an ear of corn and nodded at the other three children. CoraMarie, sensing their confusion and fright, spoke softly, touching them and even hugging Cookie when she finished her doll.

The trip to the hospital with a box full of corn shuck dolls was totally silent, and the return trip was punctuated only by sniffles and the rustle of a single doll one girl insisted on giving back to Eva, "Because," the girl said, "then you'll have one just like mine!"

So it's a quiet Saturday morning here in Cedar Gap. The town Christmas tree is glittering nicely. The old Rockola jukebox in the Palace Cafe features Willie mumbling about the virtues of roasted chestnuts, while Merle is detailing the totally unbelievable story of a mutant deer with a stoplight nose.

And over at CoraMarie Minson's house four kids are quietly eating their pancakes and bacon. Occasionally they glance at each other. But mostly they peer silently

at the corn-shuck doll sitting placidly in the center of the table.

Peace on earth. For the Gallart children, it's a first.

Reprinted by permission of the author

Jacqueline Siglin taught middle school in Alaska before moving with her husband to West Texas. She lives near Alpine and writes short fiction.

# Faded Mistletoe

by Jacqueline Siglin

The snow fell in heaps that Christmas. Frank laughed and pulled his fiancee, Karen, under a sprig of mistletoe. He kissed her and handed her a box. "For you, my sweet," he said.

Karen tugged at the red satin ribbon tied around the dark green box. It opened with a whiff of scent. "Oh," she wrinkled her nose in appreciation. "It's the best, Frank. Everybody's talking about it."

She pulled out the slender red bottle. "Mistletoe, the perfume for lovers. I love it. Just like I love you." She dabbed a bit behind her ears, then she kissed him.

They married in June. Two years later, Sandra was born and three years after that Michael.

Frank swept her up in his arms each Christmas, kissed her, then handed her the familiar dark green box. "Mistletoe," she said when she opened it on their tenth Christmas. She set the box on the table, then kissed him.

"Hmm," he said, "your favorite."

Hmm, she thought, but didn't say it out loud. It was time for an update. The saleswoman at the department store had given her a free spritz of this year's newest scent. It was much more sophisticated, but Karen looked at Frank's happy face.

"I love it," she said. "Just like I love you."

The year Sandra married and Michael joined the Peace Corps, Karen and Frank took a Christmas cruise. He laid the green box on the breakfast table after the server brought the coffee.

"Merry Christmas," he said.

"Frank. Didn't we decide this cruise was our gift to each other?"

"But it's your favorite. You love it."

"Just like I love you." She smiled, then slipped the unopened box onto her lap.

"Is that Mistletoe?" The woman sitting next to Karen asked.

"It is," Frank said.

"I'm amazed you could find it," she said. "It's not as popular as it once was."

"Anything for my girl." Frank leaned close and kissed Karen on the cheek.

Sandra caught Karen pouring the contents of two slender red bottles into the bathroom sink one afternoon while Frank was taking the grandchildren to the park.

"What you doing, Mom?" she asked. "Isn't that your perfume?"

Karen shook her head. "It's your father's perfume. Have you ever smelled anything so sickening sweet?"

She waved an empty bottle under Sandra's nose. "He doesn't have much imagination when it comes to presents. I've even walked him by the perfume counter at the store and mentioned a different label, but he's stuck on Mistletoe. I don't even know where he buys it."

The snow lay in heaps that December. Frank's grave was covered. Karen paced the house looking for something to do before she went to Sandra's for Christmas dinner. She decided to tackle Frank's closet. Maybe she'd find something to take to the grandchildren.

The sealed cardboard box was hidden in the back corner. Karen pulled it out, cut through the heavy tape and removed the lid. Five dark green boxes nestled at the bottom.

She couldn't stop the tears. They flowed down her cheeks as she lifted out a box and undid the satin ribbon. She opened the slender red bottle, dabbed the perfume behind her ears, felt the scent hold her close.

"I love it, Frank," she whispered. "Just like I love you."

Published by permission of the author

*John Erickson, creator and author of the popular* Hank the Cowdog *books, lives on a ranch nearly forty miles from Perryton in the Texas Panhandle.*

# The Solo Must Go On

by John Erickson

Getting out of this canyon to attend church in the wintertime is sometimes an ordeal. The Saturday before Christmas of 1997, a cold norther blew into the Panhandle. The weather forecasters were predicting freezing rain and snow. They got the first half of it right. It started raining in the afternoon and it rained enough to turn our ranch roads into mush.

After dark, the temperature dropped into the twenties and the rain continued. When I got up on Sunday morning, everything in sight wore a fresh coat of ice—thick ice. Uh oh. Under ordinary circumstances, we

would have called Barbara Richardson, our choir direc-
tor, and told her that we couldn't make it to church.

But today was a different deal. The choir was scheduled to present our Christmas cantata. It was to be the
whole service. And guess who had the soprano solo? My
wife, Kris. She had been rehearsing it for weeks, and yes,
we would get there. Or try.

We had the right vehicle for the trip, a three-quarter
ton four-wheel drive Suburban that had plowed that old
road to town many times. But I knew we would have to
go the Long Way to town. The Short Way, a thirty-nine
mile drive, required that we climb the caprock on a dirt
road that passed through the Tandy ranch.

That hill was steep, and when it had a coat of ice on
top, it was more than a little scary. There was a deep
canyon on the right, and no guard rail, and sliding down
it backwards offered a kind of thrill we sure didn't need.
Henry Hale and I tried that once in his four-wheel-drive
Dodge pickup. When all four wheels were turning forward and we were sliding backward down that long hill,
I took an oath not to do it again.

So we had to go the Long Way—nineteen miles of
dirt road that followed the Canadian River to Highway
70. From there, it was thirty miles of black-top to town.

The first challenge came when I tried to open the
Suburban door. It was coated with thick ice and frozen

shut. I banged and kicked on it, and finally had to pry it open with a shovel. I fired up the diesel engine, always loud and smoky on cold mornings, and started chipping away at the ice on the windshield.

By the time I accomplished that task, Kris and son Mark were bundled up in their Drive to Town wardrobe and ready to go. In the wintertime, we set out on trips looking like a band of Eskimos. Out here, you dress with the idea that you might have to walk several miles or spend the night in the car.

We loaded up and left the ranch at 9:00. In clear weather, the trip took forty-five minutes. I figured that today, we would need an hour and a half or two hours. We were supposed to be in the choir room at 10:30. The service started at 11:00. Kris's solo came in the middle of the cantata, so if we tromped into the choir loft at 11:30, we would be all right.

The first seven miles of road proved to be nothing out of the ordinary, just the usual muddy mess that followed an inch of rain. When we got down to the river, the road had more sand in it and very little mud. I figured we could make up some time . . . until I noticed that the Suburban was sliding sideways down the middle of the road. The wet sand had turned to ice.

We poked along the next twelve miles and managed to stay between the ditches, and at last we came to

Highway 70. It was wet but free of ice, but that changed when we climbed out of the valley. Up on the flats, the prairie country was one endless unbroken sheet of ice, and that included the highway.

Three miles south of Perryton, we saw a red Suburban sitting out in a wheat field. The driver had hit a patch of ice and driven through a barbed wire fence. Any thoughts I might have had about being in a hurry sort of vanished. That could have been us.

We crept along and finally pulled up to the church at 10:30. I let Kris and Mark out at the side door and parked the Suburban in the parking lot across the street. The ice was so thick and slick, I had to skate across Baylor Street, until I finally found better footing on the church lawn.

We did the cantata and made our joyful noise to the Lord. I hope He and Barbara took notice of the effort we made to get there, because next time . . . next time, if Kris is the soloist, we'll probably do it again.

Published by permission of the author

*Loretta Fulton tells about a special Christmas dinner that a Stamford church has been hosting for twenty-five years. The tradition continues.*

# More Than a Meal

by Loretta Fulton

Quite a few families in Stamford will be observing a traditional Christmas again this year, but their idea of "traditional" may be a little different from the norm.

For many in town, this will be the twenty-sixth year to stay up much of Christmas Eve or get up really early Christmas morning to help with the annual Christmas dinner at St. John's United Methodist Church.

The Gary and Connie Decker family is typical. "Our kids don't know any different," said Connie Decker.

The Decker "kids" are now twenty-nine, twenty-three, and eighteen years old. Once again, they will join a large group of St. John's members, as well as other folks in the community, to serve Christmas dinner to about 600 people, including meals delivered to shut-ins.

The Christmas dinner originated with former Stamford residents Jack and Margaret Vaughn, Decker said, as a way of getting a holiday meal to people who rely on Meals on Wheels. From there, it has grown into a community event that folks in Stamford and surrounding towns look forward to.

People who come aren't necessarily in need of a good meal, but are in need of companionship on Christmas. "There are people who are just lonely or don't have anyone," Decker said.

Work on the dinner starts early in the week before Christmas, with thirty turkeys being baked and people bringing in pans of cornbread for twenty-four large trays of dressing.

On Christmas Eve, a crew will start preparing and cooking trays of sweet potatoes and huge pots of green beans flavored with salt pork. Decker said the dinner has grown from a church project to one that draws help from practically everyone in the community, including many businesses.

When Christmas fell on Sunday in 2011, St. John's pastor, the Rev. John Erwin, saw a unique opportunity. He didn't deliver a sermon that morning. Instead, the Christmas dinner *was* the sermon.

"There is no greater message than serving other people," he said. "It's a family affair for everyone."

No one knows that better than the Decker clan. Connie Decker said she and her husband started getting their children involved as soon as they were old enough. The children—son James and daughters Jessica and Rebecca—started by going with their parents to deliver meals to shut-ins. Then they graduated to cutting pies and eventually learned how to do it all.

James Decker now practices law in Stamford, but even when he was an undergraduate at Texas A&M and in law school at Texas Tech, he always took part in the Christmas dinner.

He remembers learning from delivering meals with his dad that not everyone has a storybook Christmas. Taking meals to shut-ins and visiting with them made a huge impression on him as a youngster.

"I wanted to be like my dad," he said. "My goal in life is to help with this thing as long as I'm able."

Reprinted by permission, the *Abilene Reporter-News*

*Author and humorist Dr. Don Newbury graduated from Howard Payne University in 1961, served as the university's president from 1985-1997, and has been chancellor ever since. For more see his website, speakerdoc.com.*

# Uncle Cecil

by Don Newbury

More than a half-century has passed since some college friends and I experienced the unbounded love resulting from "special deliveries" of gifts for children in selected Brownwood homes on three consecutive Christmas Eves.

"Stars" of the gifting were Gibson's Discount Center, the Brownwood Police Department, and Uncle Cecil Holman, African-American undertaker/grocer/radio personality who was the conscience of his community. He was as admired and respected as any person I've ever known.

Making it happen was Neal Guthrie, a fellow student at Howard Payne University in Brownwood. At the time, he was a part-time employee at Gibson's. As new toys were received, any that were blemished or sub-par in any way went into a bin designated for "Uncle Cecil's kids." Over the course of half a dozen weeks, literally hundreds of toys filled the bin. Most of them were repaired with minimal effort and soon were declared good as new.

Around Thanksgiving, we checked with Holman to determine addresses of children to receive gifts, and as the days toward Christmas wound down, there would be several dozen addresses on the list.

There was a three-vehicle procession for gift delivery around 9 p.m. on Christmas Eve. Leading the way was Uncle Cecil, putting along in an old car likely taken in as payment for a funeral. Second in the line it was one of Brownwood's finest on a three-wheel motorcycle, with Santa (me) decked out in red and white riding on the back of the vehicle. Bringing up the rear was a carload of students to help distribute the gifts. (In those days, it was rare for college students to have cars, and when they did, the vehicles were old—the kind Uncle Cecil often had to reluctantly accept in lieu of cash for burials.) "There's a difference in a funeral and a burial," he'd explain. "At funerals, some money changes hands, but at burials, there sometimes are trade-ins at best, and I join 'em in the crying."

Uncle Cecil would rap on the recipients' doors, and scenes of joyous laughter followed. More wide-eyed than the children were parents who didn't know what was going on, but their broad smiles suggested total approval.

Somehow, memories of those "give-away Christmas Eves" stand out, proof, of course, that it is more blessed to give than to receive. (Someone else said, "Don't give 'til it hurts, give 'til it feels good!") This project felt really good.

Within a few years, Neal Guthrie owned a Gibson's store in Stephenville, where to this day he's a leading citizen, long married to his wife, Sharon, who also attended Howard Payne. Within a decade or so, Uncle Cecil was gone, finally claimed by diabetes that had been a life-long challenge. No doubt the policeman is gone, too, and the three-wheeled motorcycle went to the junk yard decades ago.

I don't remember other students' names, but I'd wager that they, like Neal and me, have told the story many, many times of our little Christmas project involving Gibson's, an undertaker, and the police department.

My only regret is that I didn't blacken my face and hands in my role as Santa. It simply never occurred to me that it would clearly have been the right thing to do. Uncle Cecil probably thought about it, and would

have endorsed the thought had it originated with someone else. He never suggested it, though, fearful of being
misunderstood. That's the kind of man he was—giving,
always giving, and always good for a joke.

In the evenings, he was a disc jockey on a Brownwood
radio station. One of the sponsors was the Holman "coast
to coast" funeral service. In those days, funeral homes
provided ambulance service, too. Uncle Cecil joked that
his ambulance was "fully equipped with May-Pop tires,"
explaining they were so thin, they "may pop" around any
corner. He also vowed that many of his "patients" were
folks who didn't have money for cab fare.

I closed out many nights during college visiting Uncle
Cecil at his little grocery store in what locals called "the
flats." I watched him extend credit, give food away, and
offer counsel to folks coming through the front door.
Some came for the counseling with intent; others got it
anyway. I learned much.

I have three university degrees and post-doctoral
study and have sat at the feet of many wonderful teachers.
None was better, though, than Uncle Cecil Holman, my
friend who never finished high school, but was as wise
as anyone I ever knew.

Who is to say that we aren't in the presence of saints
from time to time? If I have been so privileged, it was
while in the company of "St. Cecil." He somehow "loved

everybody," at Christmas time and throughout the year. I miss him greatly, this Christian giant who addressed me always as "Mr. Berries." Would that everyone could be privileged to have such a model for life.

Published by permission of the author

Marla Cooper of Odessa remembers a Christmas thirty years ago when a popular holiday song took on a new meaning.

# Chestnuts Roasting

by Marla Cooper

Back in the '80s, when there was no Internet to consult, things were not so predictable. This must have happened around 1983 after my mother-in-law and I had finally become friends. She was young and silly like me, and we both enjoyed drinking wine. Plus, we were both West Texas ladies. Neither of us knew any better.

I'd gone to the store and found among the bins of Christmas nuts, the very treat that epitomized the season: *chestnuts.* So, along with a couple of bottles of Chardonnay, I bought two pounds thinking I'd take them to her house. Then, just like I'd seen on television, we'd roast them, slather them with butter and celebrate the season.

Only one problem: no open fire like the song says. Still, she was a good cook. She'd figure a way to cook those little dudes.

I got to her house and explained my plans. "Why, we'll just roast them like anything else," she said. So, into the ten-inch cast-iron skillet they went. She set the oven at 350 degrees and put them in. While she'd been busy with that, I had poured the wine.

We sat down to enjoy our libations and talk about the holidays: who was going where and who was hoping for this or that. We talked about clothes and what we were going to wear to the big party coming up. We talked about my twenty-two-month-old son, off with his daddy doing man stuff, and what we were going to get each of them for Christmas.

We talked about the past and the future. I poured more wine. We laughed and put on some music. We talked about parents and parenting. We talked about brothers and sisters. We talked about my sister-in-law. We talked and talked.

I opened the second bottle and refilled our glasses. It must have been after that second bottle had been poured, because both of us were really enjoying the afternoon, when the first muffled BOOM startled us. We looked at each other with big eyes wondering where that noise had come from. The second BOOM blew the door of the oven open just a little and we realized what was happening. Our chestnuts were exploding like big brown kernels of popcorn!

We started laughing. At our ignorance. At our surprise. At each other.

Another BOOM reminded us to turn off the oven, but for God's sake, don't open that oven door. Two pounds of chestnuts is a lot. Even after we had turned the fire off, they continued to burst and with every explosion we laughed harder and harder.

I don't remember what happened after that, but to this day, the line "Chestnuts roasting on an open fire" has a special meaning for me and one other silly old woman living in West Texas.

Published by permission of the author

*A. C. Greene grew up in Abilene and went on to become well known in Texas literary circles. Every year the Friends of the Abilene Public Library give the A. C. Greene Literary Award to a distinguished Texas author. Greene's book about the* Santa Claus Bank Robbery, *first published in 1972, is still available from* University of North Texas Press. *He also wrote a short piece about the 1927 robbery in a book of* Texas Sketches. *That account is published here.*

# The Santa Claus Bank Robbery

by A. C. Greene

On December 23, 1927, Santa Claus and three helpers set out to rob a bank. It happened in Cisco, Texas and became the most bizarre bank robbery in American history.

The four men held up the First National Bank, the leader wearing the Santa mask and suit because Cisco had been his home and he was well known there. He thought in the Christmas season a Santa Claus outfit would be a perfect disguise.

From the beginning the episode was a comedy of errors—and death.

A little girl saw "Santa Claus" enter the bank and she dragged her mother along so she could tell Santa one last wish. When she and her mother entered the front door of the bank and saw men with drawn guns, the girl started crying, "They're going to kill Santa Claus!" and because the hold-up men weren't hard-hearted enough to harm them, the mother and the girl ran through the bank and out a rear door, screaming the alarm.

Spurred by a well publicized $5,000 "Dead Bank Robber" reward, offered by Texas bankers, within minutes the bank was surrounded by armed citizens, some of whom had gone into hardware stores and grabbed up guns from stock.

The robbers shot their way through the ambush to their getaway car, stolen the night before, only to discover within a couple of miles that the gasoline gauge was showing empty. They had forgotten to fill the tank after driving the stolen vehicle from Wichita Falls.

Then, when they held up another car in order to take it, the fourteen-year-old driver calmly pocketed the ignition keys and walked away and hid. An armed posse was right on their tails, so the robbers jumped back in the first car and fled again—in their rush leaving behind a dying companion and everything they had taken in the robbery.

By that time not only was one of them dying, two Cisco policemen, including the chief, were dead. The manhunt that ensued was the biggest in Texas history, involving several sheriffs, dozens of citizens, and the Texas Rangers under the famous Captain Tom (Ace) Hickman. This was the first time the Rangers used an airplane in a search, sending Ranger M. T. (Lone Wolf) Gonzaullas aloft in an open cockpit plane to scour a section of Brazos River bottoms near Graham. It took a week for the three remaining hold-up men to be caught.

Ultimately, one of the robbers was given life, one was electrocuted, and on November 19, 1929, after he had mortally wounded a jailer, a mob broke into the Eastland County jail, pulled out "Santa Claus" and lynched him, so that eventually six men died from Cisco's grim Christmas crime caper.

Published by permission of the A. C. Greene Estate

*Burle Pettit, editor emeritus of the* Lubbock Avalanche-Journal, *grew up in Moran and wrote about a Christmas he remembered there. The piece originally ran in the* Avalanche-Journal.

# Fire Truck Santa

by Burle Pettit

Only twice a year was Main Street roped off and closed to traffic. One of those occasions was Christmas Eve, which this night happened to be.

My excitement and anticipation mounted as I watched Santa Claus himself—obviously the real Santa—emerge from Doc Martin's drug store and climb slowly up onto the fire truck which had been backed to the curb near the entry.

That night in midtown Moran happened long ago—I was maybe five or six at the time—and it didn't actually occur on Main Street, that's simply what all the locals called it, even those who knew it actually was Fisher Street. But because that was the center of trade and all other activities, it was, indeed, the main street of a town that never had got around to putting up street signs.

Of all the memories—good and bad, joyous and sad, lonely and warmly surrounded—that night requires a description all its own: It was shockingly traumatic.

Looking back on it now, what ol' Santa brought to our house that year was probably nothing more than a rubber ball or a toy automobile. But I was almost as proud of the new shirt that Mom had manufactured herself, working with a needle, thread, and thimble when I was out of her sight. I imagined Santa had stitched it himself.

From our parents, Mom especially, we heard a lot about the spirit of Christmas, the reason for Christmas and about all the people less fortunate than we. It didn't occur to me to wonder who in the world they could have been.

Without Expectations as a sire, Disappointment was never birthed. The joyous surroundings provided by a houseful of brothers and sisters, a loving mom, and an amazingly resourceful dad emitted a familial warmth whose memory lingers still.

But I digress.

Each year when Santa climbed aboard that fire truck in downtown Moran, he faced an audience of youngsters that flocked around all three accessible sides of his bright red stage.

Having seen a number of his "helpers" appear in full uniform at school and elsewhere, I was convinced that this man was the real deal.

His beard clung tightly to his face, which was warm and wrinkled and clearly not a mask, and his gravel voice had no doubt been developed by driving and directing Dancer and Prancer and Donner and Vixen . . . and—hey, I could have named all eight (Gene Autry had not yet given birth to Rudolph).

From his large red bag, Santa retrieved candy and nuts and apples and oranges, which he tossed to the throng of moppets below.

On that night, my vantage was from Dad's shoulders, straddling his neck. My own hands were outstretched, but I knew he also was ready to grab whatever was tossed our way.

Then, with unexpected suddenness, ol' Santa—in an attempt to reach a youngster at the fringe of the crowd—leaned over too far and crashed headfirst onto the pavement below.

My heart leaped to my throat as Dad passed me immediately to an older brother and scurried off to help. Fortunately, Doc Forrester's office was in the back of the drug store and he was standing nearby when it happened.

En route home, Dad assured me that Santa was well and, after the doctor patched his head, he had hopped aboard his sled and continued on his way.

A few days later, I was visiting my friend Brit and noticed that his father, Sam—a rather portly man with a flock of long, white hair—had a large bandage covering much of his head. When I asked what happened, Brit replied that he had fallen off a fire truck.

"Wow," I thought. "What a coincidence."

Reprinted courtesy of the *Lubbock Avalanche-Journal*

*Religion editor Beth Pratt had a Santa Claus experience at a Baptist gathering in 1996. She wrote about it in her weekly column in the* Lubbock Avalanche-Journal.

# Santa Claus a Baptist?

by Beth Pratt

Santa Claus always came to our house on Christmas Eve when I was a child.

In the early darkness of a cold, winter day, we would sit on the floor around the open-flame heater and do whatever it is children do to contain their excitement and try to be good.

I would cut out paper dolls from the Sears-Roebuck catalog or draw and color my own paper playmates while my two younger brothers played nearby with their toys. As it got darker outside, Dad would read "Twas the Night Before Christmas" to us, and ask us to listen with him to see if we could hear reindeer on the roof. Mother was usually in the kitchen creating wonderful food to take to the big family Christmas Day dinner.

Dad told us that the jolly elf would not appear as long as we were watching, so it was not hard to persuade us to shut the three doors to the living room and move our play into the kitchen and adjoining bedroom.

Once, we went for a short drive. We had no fireplace or chimney, so it seems an aunt stayed to open the door should Santa knock, and our uncle went along to drive. When we returned home our aunt had gone on home, but Santa had made his visit.

When my parents weren't watching, I did try to peek through the keyhole to spy on Santa Claus, but I never did get a glimpse of the elusive fellow. Long ago, I had given up all hope of actually meeting Santa Claus face to face.

Years later, I was away from home working, not even thinking about Christmas, much less Santa.

Then, what to my wandering adult eyes should appear in downtown Fort Worth but a cherubic, white-bearded visage so familiar I halted in mid-step. Busy about his own affairs, the gentleman paid no attention as I impolitely stared.

In mid-November you might expect the jolly saint to be stashed away atop the North Pole, twice-checking his lists of addresses for good boys and girls. Instead, he was hurrying from a meeting of—are you ready for this—Baptists.

Santa Claus a Baptist? How could that be?

As the man drew closer, I realized he was very little taller than I. And, yes, the eyes were merry. The thick, white hair on his head was complemented by an impeccably-groomed white, fluffy, curly beard and mustache.

All I can tell you about his clothing is that he was not wearing red, but some nondescript brown sport coat. Tie or not, I do not remember, but I think not.

Having given up meeting the fellow in person, and yes, I must admit, having doubted his existence, I had given no thought to what I would say should our paths ever cross.

Besides, I had always assumed he would look like he had popped off a Christmas card so that I would know for sure who he was. I had not thought that he might live and work throughout the year much as the rest of us do.

My PRESS tag was prominently displayed on my jacket, so giving him my best reporter smile, I stepped right up to him and said, "You must be Santa Claus."

He stopped, obviously not surprised at my question. He had heard it all before.

"I'm a music minister on staff at a church near here," he said, reaching into his pocket and pulling out a card that he put in my hand as he hurried on his way. I, too, was rushing to cover another story at the Baptist General Convention of Texas annual meeting.

But I paused to look at the card. There he was on the card, eyes peering through gold-rimmed spectacles, dressed in the traditional red fur-trimmed suit with a white-gloved ginger across his lips in the "sh-h-h, don't tell" signal. At the bottom of the card was the name "Santa Claus." Below, instead of an address at the North Pole, was the word "Metro," followed by a telephone number.

After I got home, I called. Another surprise. Santa had an answering machine. I left my name and number. Would he call me back? I figured I'd better get my list ready just in case.

Reprinted courtesy of the *Lubbock Avalanche-Journal*

*This piece was included in a collection of stories published in book form as* A Small Town in Texas.

# The First Time I Saw Santa

by Glenn Dromgoole

Can you remember the first time you saw Santa Claus? I do. Well, not the first time I looked at Santa or sat in Santa's lap or gazed into Santa's beard. I don't remember those.

But I do remember the first time I really *saw* Santa.

I'm not sure how old I was, probably six or seven, and I'm fairly sure at the time I didn't realize what I had seen. That would come later.

I do remember it was a Christmas Eve, and it was after dark. We were in a hurry to leave town and drive to my grandparents' farm house where there would be cousins to play with, good things to eat, and plenty of presents.

We usually didn't leave for their house until after noon on Christmas Eve, frequently not until after dark. That time it wasn't until after dark.

My dad had been working all day helping deliver baskets of food and toys to the needy families in our town. That day, as I remember it, all the deliveries had been made but one.

There was a house a couple of miles outside of town where a struggling young couple lived with their children—I'm not sure how many.

Dad said he would deliver the food and toys to that home before we headed out of town. We stopped outside the shack where the family lived. We waited in the car while dad went inside.

For some reason he decided to put on a Santa suit he had used earlier in the Christmas season—at the church Christmas program or as the town's Santa arriving on the fire truck. He was wearing the Santa suit as he stepped out of the car and started making his way to the shanty.

As he approached the house, the children—who no doubt had been told by their parents not to expect anything for Christmas that year—saw him coming.

They began to jump and shout for joy. Santa was at the doorstep. And he had presents for *them.* Santa had not forgotten.

"I told you he would come!" the oldest brother shrieked. "I told you he would come!"

That was the first time I saw Santa.

Reprinted by permission, State House Press

*This parody was published in the* El Paso Times *on Christmas Day for about thirty years, from 1948 to 1977. Sent in to longtime editor William J. Hooten by a reader, the author of the poem is unknown, according to* Times *archivist Trish Long, although at least once it was attributed to a Guillermo Lobato, which may have been a pen name.*

# Merry Christmas Amigos

Author Unknown

'Tis the night before Christmas, and all through the casa
Not a creature is stirring. Caramba! Que Pasa?
The stockings are hanging, con mucho cuidado,
In hopes that St. Nicholas will feel obligado
To leave a few cosas aqui and alli,
For chico and chica (and something for me!)
Los ninos are snuggled all safe in their camas
(Some in camisas and some in pajamas.)

Their little cabezas are full of good things
Todos esperan lo que Santa will bring!
Santa is down at the corner saloon
(Muy borracho since mid-afternoon);
Mama is sitting beside the ventana
Shining her rolling pin para mañana
When Santa will come en un manner extraño,
Lit up like the Star on the mountain, cantando,
Y mama lo manda to bed with a right.
Merry Christmas a todos y a todos good night!

# Stable Gifts for Today: A Benediction

*Please join us at the stable, where we have come searching for meaning on this special day.*

After the presents are opened, and the songs sung, and the dinner enjoyed, we look around to find the lasting gifts of today are not under the tree, but are here, in a simple and familiar stable:

The *love* of a parent.

The *life* of an infant.

The *promise* of an angel.

The *faith* of a shepherd.

The *generosity* of a wise man.

The *guidance* of a star.

The *peace* and *joy* and *hope* of a Christmas.

May these gifts be yours today and throughout the year.

Merry Christmas.

*Glenn Dromgoole*

# About the Author

Glenn Dromgoole, former editor of the *Abilene Reporter-News*, is the author of twenty-six books. A native Texan, he has lived in West Texas for nearly three decades and is founder of the West Texas Book Festival held every September in Abilene. He and his wife Carol own Texas Star Trading Company, a Texas book, gift, and gourmet shop in Abilene (texasstartrading.com). His website is www.glenndromgoole.com.